PASSION FOR
PEACE

PASSION FOR
PEACE

Reflections on War
and Nonviolence

THOMAS MERTON

Edited and with an Introduction by
William H. Shannon

A Crossroad Book
The Crossroad Publishing Company
New York

The Crossroad Publishing Company
16 Penn Plaza – 481 Eighth Avenue, Suite 1550
New York, NY 10001

This is an abridged edition of **Passion for Peace: The Social Essays,**
first published by The Crossroad Publishing Company in 1995.

Printed in the United States of America.

The text of this book is set in 11/15 Sabon.
The display face is Futura.

Library of Congress Cataloging-in-Publication Data

Merton, Thomas, 1915-1968.
    Passion for peace : reflections on war and nonviolence / Thomas Merton ;
with an introduction by William H. Shannon. – Abridged ed.
       p.   cm.
    Includes index.
    ISBN-13: 978-0-8245-2415-9 (alk. paper)
    ISBN-10: 0-8245-2415-2 (alk. paper)
    1. Peace – Religious aspects – Catholic Church. 2. Nonviolence – Religious
aspects – Catholic Church. 3. Race relations – Religious aspects – Catholic
Church. 4. United States – Race relations. 5. Merton, Thomas, 1915-1968.
6. Catholic Church – Clergy – Biography. I. Shannon, William Henry, 1917-
II. Title.
BX1795.P43M47 2006
261.8'73 – dc22

                                                                                    2006016422

1   2   3   4   5   6   7   8   9   10   12   11   10   09   08   07   06

Contents

Contents

Introduction to the Original Edition

Life is a struggle; indeed it is often a series of struggles. People's true characters, in great measure, come to the fore in the way they handle the struggles unique to their lives. One way of coming to some understanding of Thomas Merton's character is by looking at the struggles his life brought him and seeing his character brought into clearer focus by the ways he dealt with them. In his earliest years he struggled to make sense out of life. This struggle, which took nearly half his life, found its initial resolution in his conversion to Christian faith and, just three years later, his entrance into the Abbey of Gethsemani. Once in the monastery, the ongoing quest for meaning took on new guises. He agonized for some years over his obvious talent as a writer and the threat it posed — or so he thought for some time — to his contemplative vocation. Another tension he had to face was the call he experienced — or seemed to be experiencing — to a deeper solitude. He felt drawn to transfer to a hermit order such as the Carthusians or the Camaldolese; and yet his sense of belonging to Gethsemani was strong. Later in his monastic life, he underwent a sense of estrangement from the structures of monasticism and the need to rethink what it meant to be a monk in the twentieth century and in the wake of the Second Vatican Council. On this issue of monastic reform, he was often at odds — and in substantive ways — with his more conservative abbot, Dom James Fox. It was an uncomfortable position to be in, first because Merton believed firmly in monastic obedience, and second because he had a sincere affection for Dom James, despite the fact that they were often at cross-purposes on various matters of monastic life.

These and other struggles that help to make the Merton story an absorbing one have been detailed in the various biographical studies that have been published. There is one struggle that I think has not been given as much attention as it deserves. Merton faced it in 1961; I think it is safe to say he agonized over it throughout that year and the next and actually never set it aside. The struggle, simply stated, was this: Should I, a monk of Gethsemani vowed to silence and solitude, speak out against the terrible violence of war that threatens the very life of the planet, or should I keep a discreet silence as the appropriate stance for a monk?

It is not easy for us to grasp the anguish that this struggle posed for Merton. It was a new question for a monk, indeed a new question for almost any Christian of the day. We live at a time when it is not an uncommon thing for Roman Catholics to protest against war and to lobby for peace. Pax Christi USA has been in existence for more than twenty years. Many dioceses and parishes in the Roman Catholic Church have peace and justice committees that are alive and active. But in 1961, things were much different. At that time no Catholic priest or bishop — at least none well known — had spoken out against war. Roman Catholics by and large were a patriotic lot. I remember a bishop of that time who in a public talk echoed the words of Stephen Decatur, the naval officer in the war of 1812 who said, "Our country . . . may she always be in the right. But our country, right or wrong." Thirty years ago a Roman Catholic bishop could get away with such a statement. Today such a crude nationalism on the part of a bishop would be intolerable, even scandalous.

Think of Thomas Merton living in that kind of religious and civic climate. Remember the reputation he had. A well-known Catholic priest and monk, he was looked to as an inspiring writer on spirituality. In Catholic circles no one rivaled him in prominence or influence. His earliest writings, especially his best-selling autobiography, *The Seven Storey Mountain,* had praised a spirituality of withdrawal from the world. Who of his thousands of readers could have anticipated that Merton, of all people, would ever start writing — and writing with deep passion — on such a worldly subject as war? Some of his many readers were scandalized and walked with him no more. Others shook their heads and asked themselves, "What in the world has happened to Thomas Merton? Why is he calling people to unite in a crusade to abolish all war? What does this have to do with his spirituality?"

Well, by 1961 quite a lot had happened to Thomas Merton, and he was quite certain that what he had said about spirituality had a great deal to do with the social problems of the day and especially with the issue of war. What had happened to him was that his solitude had issued into what all true solitude must eventually become: compassion. Finding God in his solitude, he found God's people, who are inseparable from God and who, at the deepest level of their being (the level that only contemplation can reach), are at one with one another in God, the Hidden Ground of Love of all that is. This sense of compassion bred in solitude (something like the *karuna* of the Buddha born of his enlightenment) moved him to look once again at the world he thought he had left irrevocably twenty years earlier, in 1941, when he had entered the monastery. He now felt a duty, *precisely because he was a contemplative,* to speak out and to warn his fellow men and women about what he believed was the gravest possible danger threatening the civilized world.

He confided his concern to Daniel Berrigan in a letter written on June 25, 1963: "What is the contemplative life if one does not listen to God in it? What is the contemplative life if one becomes oblivious to the rights of men and the truth of God in the world and in His Church?" (*Hidden Ground of Love*, 79)

Merton felt that, however poorly equipped he might be for the role, he was called to be a prophet. He understood clearly the limitations of the prophet's vocation. A prophet is not necessarily one who has all the right answers; he or she *is* the one who knows at a given moment in history what the real problems are that humanity must face, what the proper goals are that need to be achieved, what the right questions are that must be asked. In a passage from *Conjectures of a Guilty Bystander* Merton offers a perceptive explanation for the popularity of his writings. "It seems to me that one of the reasons why my writings appeal to many people is precisely that I am not so sure of myself and do not claim to have all the answers" (p. 49). In his writings on war and peace, it is passion for the goals he sees rather than certitude about the way to achieve them that dominates. There were times that he felt lonely, diffident, distrustful of himself, even shocked by some of the things he heard himself saying. His concern lest he lead people in wrong directions shows up in his sensitivity to criticism, his apologies for over-hasty statements, his constant rewriting of articles to make his intent clearer and, he hoped, more palatable to his readers. Yet despite his misgivings about himself and his message, despite his concern about the abdication of responsibility on the part of so many of his fellow citizens, he knew that he had to continue, with whatever means at his disposal, to combat war and to work for the creation of a stable and lasting peace. Commenting on the prison writings of Father Delp, he says:

> Christ our Lord did not come to bring peace as a kind of spiritual tranquilizer. He brought to his disciples a vocation and a task: to struggle in the world of violence to establish His peace not only in their own hearts but in society itself.

These were his marching orders. He had no choice but to obey.

Merton's contribution to this struggle to establish God's peace in a world of violence was, I believe, threefold: (1) his passionate commitment, in article after article, to the position that war must be totally outlawed; (2) his discernment of the way in which war must be opposed, namely, through nonviolence; and (3) his widening of the area in which nonviolence must operate. Nonviolence is not just a stance toward war; it is a way of life that affects everything we do. Merton knew well the meaning of nonviolence. He had learned it from a master. One might expect that that master would have been Jesus Christ. Actually, it was Mohandas Gandhi. If Merton eventually found the nonviolence of Jesus in the Gospels (as I believe he did), he learned it from this strange-looking, quaint little man, whose nonviolence and effective civil disobedience won the world's somewhat bewildered respect as well as the independence of his native India. Merton read Gandhi's writings carefully and was able to articulate clearly and firmly what nonviolence involves. In the articles that make up this book, there is much wisdom about nonviolence; it is a wisdom that we very much need today as we strive to cope with the violence in our own hearts as well as the violence that wracks our cities and paralyzes so many countries in such diverse parts of the world.

This brings me back to a fundamental thesis of this introduction, namely, that Merton's writings on social issues flowed from a deep contemplative vision. I have the strong conviction that we shall learn to deal effectively with violence only when we discover (or recover, for it is really always there) in ourselves that contemplative awareness that enables us — as it had enabled Merton — to see the oneness we share with all God's people, indeed with the whole of God's creation. Once a person has achieved this contemplative insight, nonviolence ceases to be a mere option and becomes a choice that brooks no rejection. But let no one think that becoming nonviolent is an easy task. It calls for painful, ongoing conversion, as slowly and almost imperceptibly we begin to realize what it asks of us and to experience the wisdom it imparts to us.

This volume contains a selection of Merton's writings on war and peace. In these essays he pleads the case against nuclear war. His task, he felt, was to help people see that peace is indeed a viable possibility in our world. He had to expose for the terrible illusion that it is the Great Lie of history, which says that war is inevitable and permanent peace an unrealizable dream.

The historical context in which Merton wrote was that of the Cold War, a term coined by Walter Lippman to express the political and military standoff between the United States and the Union of Soviet Socialist Republics. It was a standoff that had reached an especially difficult point of tension in the early 1960s. For instance, it was the year 1962 that witnessed the confrontation between President John F. Kennedy and the Soviet premier, Nikita Khrushchev, over missile sites in Cuba.

With the breakup of the Soviet Union, it might seem at first reflection, that the Cold War has come to an end. Would this mean, we cannot help but ask, that Merton's writings dealing with the Cold War are now of a purely historical interest and have nothing to say to us today? I think not. The Cold War, it seems clear, is still very much with us. The protagonists may have changed, but the reality is very much present. It is worth pointing out that the *American Heritage Dictionary,* in its 1992 edition, defines "cold war" in terms much more general than those originally used by Walter Lippman: "a state of political tension and military rivalry between nations that stops short of full-scale war." It even offers a meaning that involves groups smaller than nations: "a state of rivalry and tension between two factions, groups, or individuals that stops short of open, violent confrontation."

The violence that exists in so many places throughout the world — the murders that violate the safety of our city streets; the bloody wars that have taken thousands of lives; the ongoing tensions that continue to create a volatile instability in the Middle East; the genocide, the ethnic "cleansing" that goes on in Africa, the former Yugoslavia, and elsewhere — makes clear to us that "cold war" (and hot war, too) is very much with us today. The need to overcome war and the threat of war, the duty to work for peace in today's world remains a huge responsibility that we ignore at our own peril. And what is imperiled is not only the well-being of humankind but also our own authenticity.

Some of the things that Merton has to say on these issues are dated and probably only of historical and biographical interest. But I hasten to add that so much that he wrote speaks penetratingly to our own time. There is a certain perennial quality to his writing that gives it power to move us today. It is as if, in so many of these articles, he is actually writing today. He is speaking to us.

This is true not only of his writing on war, but also on racial issues. In his writings about civil rights for both Afro-Americans and Native Americans, he addresses an issue that still remains largely unresolved today. Once again it is the contemplative who is able to point out to us the essential oneness that roots the equal dignity of all peoples. Merton, I believe, would have agreed with the sign I remember seeing scrawled on a wall in Andersonville, the Catholic section of Belfast, Ireland. It said: "If one of us is deprived of liberty, none of us is free."

I have arranged the essays in this book in two unequal parts. The first part I am calling "The Year of the *Cold War Letters.*" As I have explained in my biography of Merton, *Silent Lamp,* this is not a calendar year, but a period that extends from October 1961 to October 1962. I have so named it because Merton selected 111 letters he had written during this twelve-month period, had them mimeographed, and sent them to his friends under the title of *Cold War Letters*. It was during this period that Merton was obsessed with the need to speak out against nuclear war. The result was that, besides the *Cold War Letters*, there was a flurry of articles on war, peace, and nonviolence. How trying a year this was for him and how he agonized over the articles he wrote will come clear, I hope, in the introductions I have written to individual articles.

The second part is called, somewhat unimaginatively I suppose, "Following the Year of the *Cold War Letters*." During this period Merton continued to write on the war issue, but much less frequently. One of the reasons for the falling-off of such articles was the directive that came to him in April of 1962 from the abbot general of the entire Cistercian order forbidding him to write anything further on this issue. There was also another factor at work. Merton was not a one-issue person. Gradually he had broadened the spectrum of the social issues he felt obligated to discuss and had begun to talk about the "cold war" (sometimes breaking into hot war) that strained the relationship of nonwhites and whites in American society.

Before closing this Introduction, I need to advise the reader that most of the articles that follow have been previously published, for example, in *Seeds of Destruction,* published by Farrar, Straus, and Giroux in 1964, and in *The Non-Violent Alternative,* a selection of articles compiled by Gordon Zahn and published by Farrar, Straus, and Giroux in 1980.

Those works were suitable for their time. They made easily accessible Merton's important articles on social issues, which many people did not even know he had written. While these books served the good purpose of unveiling another side of the monk who had spoken so eloquently on spirituality, they have one serious drawback. They fail to contextualize the many articles they include. Perhaps this was not necessary when they were first published, but, as we get to know more about Merton, we realize more and more clearly the interplay between his life and his writings. The writings shed light on his life story. His life story influenced the way the writings came into being.

In this book I have tried to supply the missing context. Properly situated historically, the articles in this book are a kind of autobiography of Merton the social critic. They portray his frequent run-ins with the censors, his concern not to be misunderstood, his ongoing fear that he had not expressed himself clearly and accurately, his compulsion to rewrite articles to make his meaning more intelligible. This background knowledge helps to make these articles come alive. They show us sides of Merton's character that simply do not come through in his other books. I hope that understanding these articles in their context will show readers a neglected side of Thomas Merton: his passion for peace and the ardor with which he pleaded for it, in a world that yearned for it so desperately.

PART ONE

The Year of the
Cold War Letters

October 1961–October 1962

– One –

The Root of War Is Fear

This article marked the initial and definitive entry of Thomas Merton into the struggle against war. Originally it was a chapter of a book Merton had been working on in early 1961, *New Seeds of Contemplation,* which would be published in January of 1962. In the late summer of 1961 Merton received approval of the censors for the publication of the book. Immediately on receiving that approval, he wrote to Dorothy Day (September 22, 1961), offering her chapter 16 of the book for publication in the *Catholic Worker.* Chapter 16 carried the title "The Root of War Is Fear" and was published in the October 1961 issue of the *Catholic Worker.* In his letter to Day he mentioned, almost casually, that he had added a page or two "to situate these thoughts in the present crisis" (*Hidden Ground of Love,* 140). This addition amounted to three long paragraphs into which Merton managed to pack a good deal of material, much of which was highly incendiary. And, of course, the addition had not been seen by the censors! In the text that follows, the uncensored paragraphs are printed first and in bold type and are followed by chapter 16 of *New Seeds of Contemplation.* The article was reprinted in the

January 1, 1962, issue of *Fellowship,* the journal of the Fellowship of Reconciliation.

The present war crisis is something we have made entirely for and by ourselves. There is in reality not the slightest logical reason for war, and yet the whole world is plunging headlong into frightful destruction, and doing so *with the purpose of avoiding war and preserving peace!* This is a true war-madness, an illness of the mind and the spirit that is spreading with a furious and subtle contagion all over the world. Of all the countries that are sick, America is perhaps the most grievously afflicted. On all sides we have people building bomb shelters where, in case of nuclear war, they will simply bake slowly instead of burning up quickly or being blown out of existence in a flash. And they are prepared to sit in these shelters with machine guns with which to prevent their neighbor from entering. This is a nation that claims to be fighting for religious truth along with freedom and other values of the spirit. Truly we have entered the "post-Christian era" with a vengeance. Whether we are destroyed or whether we survive, the future is awful to contemplate.

The Christian

What is the place of the Christian in all this? Is he simply to fold his hands and resign himself to the worst, accepting it as the inescapable will of God and preparing himself to enter heaven with a sigh of relief? Should he open up the Apocalypse and run out into the street to give everyone his idea of what is happening? Or worse still, should he take a hard-headed and "practical" attitude about it and join in the madness of the warmakers, calculating how by a "first strike" the glorious Christian West can eliminate atheistic communism for all time and usher in the millennium? ... I am no prophet and no seer but it seems to me that this last position may very well be the most diabolical of illusions, the great and not even subtle temptation of a Christianity that has grown rich and comfortable, and is satisfied with its riches.

What are we to do? The duty of the Christian in this crisis is to strive with all his power and intelligence, with his faith, hope in Christ, and love for God and man, to do the one task which God has imposed upon us in the world today. That task is to work for the total abolition of war. *There can be no question that unless war is abolished the world will remain constantly in a state of madness and desperation in which, because of the immense destructive power of modern weapons, the danger of catastrophe will be imminent and probably at every moment everywhere.* Unless we set ourselves immediately to this task, both as individuals and in our political and religious groups, we tend by our passivity and fatalism to cooperate with the destructive forces that are leading inexorably to war. It is a problem of terrifying complexity and magnitude, for which the Church herself is not fully able to see clear and decisive solutions. Yet she must lead the way on the road toward nonviolent settlement of difficulties and toward the gradual abolition of war as the way of settling international or civil disputes. Christians must become active in every possible way, mobilizing all their resources for the fight against war. First of all there is much to be studied, much to be learned. Peace is to be preached, nonviolence is to be explained as a practical method, and not left to be mocked as an outlet for crackpots who want to make a show of themselves. Prayer and sacrifice must be used as the most effective spiritual weapons in the war against war, and like all weapons they must be used with deliberate aim: not just with a vague aspiration for peace and security, but against violence and against war. This implies that we are also willing to sacrifice and restrain our own instinct for violence and aggressiveness in our relations with other people. We may never succeed in this campaign but whether we succeed or not the duty is evident. It is the great Christian task of our time. Everything else is secondary, for the survival of the human race itself depends on it. We must at least face this responsibility and do something about it. And the first job of all is to understand the psychological forces at work in ourselves and in society.

Chapter 16 (from *New Seeds of Contemplation*)

At the root of all war is fear, not so much the fear men have of one another as the fear they have of *everything*. It is not merely that they do not trust one another: they do not even trust themselves. If they are not sure when someone else may turn around and kill them, they are still less sure when they may turn around and kill themselves. They cannot trust anything, because they have ceased to believe in God.

It is not only our hatred of others that is dangerous but also and above all our hatred of ourselves: particularly that hatred of ourselves which is too deep and too powerful to be consciously faced. For it is this which makes us see our own evil in others and unable to see it in ourselves.

When we see crime in others, we try to correct it by destroying them or at least putting them out of sight. It is easy to identify the sin with the sinner when he is someone other than our own self. In ourselves, it is the other way around: we see the sin, but we have great difficulty in shouldering responsibility for it. We find it very hard to

27

identify our sin with our own will and our own malice. On the contrary, we naturally tend to interpret our immoral act as an involuntary mistake, or as the malice of a spirit in us that is other than ourselves. Yet at the same time we are fully aware that others do not make this convenient distinction for us. The acts that have been done are, in their eyes, "our" acts and they hold us fully responsible.

What is more, we tend unconsciously to ease ourselves still more of the burden of guilt that is in us, by passing it on to somebody else. When I have done wrong and have excused myself by attributing the wrong to "another" who is unaccountably "in me" my conscience is not yet satisfied. There is still too much left to be explained. The "other in myself" is too close to home. The temptation is, then, to account for my fault by seeing an equivalent amount of evil in someone else. Hence I minimize my own sins and compensate for doing so by exaggerating the faults of others.

As if this were not enough, we make the situation much worse by artificially intensifying our sense of evil, and by increasing our propensity to feel guilt even for things which are not in themselves wrong. In all these ways we build up such an obsession with evil, both in ourselves and in others, that we waste all our mental energy trying to account for this evil, to punish it, to exorcise it, or to get rid of it in any way we can.

28

We drive ourselves mad with our preoccupation, and in the end there is no outlet left but violence. We have to destroy something or someone. By that time, we have created for ourselves a suitable enemy, a scapegoat in whom we have invested all the evil in the world. He is the cause of every wrong. He is the fomenter of all conflict. If he can only be destroyed, conflict will cease, evil will be done with, there will be no more war.

This kind of fictional thinking is especially dangerous when it is supported by a whole elaborate pseudo-scientific structure of myths, like those which Marxists have adopted as their ersatz for religion. But it is certainly no less dangerous when it operates in the vague, fluid, confused, and unprincipled opportunism which substitutes in the West for religion, for philosophy, and even for mature thought.

When the whole world is in moral confusion: when no one knows any longer what to think, and when, in fact, everybody is running away from the responsibility of thinking, when man makes rational thought about moral issues absurd by exiling himself entirely from realities into the realm of fictions, and when he expends all his efforts in constructing more fictions with which to account for his ethical failures, then it becomes clear that the world cannot be saved from global war and global destruction by the mere efforts and good intentions of peacemakers. In actual fact, everyone is becoming more and more aware of the widening gulf between efforts to make peace and the growing likelihood of war. It seems that no matter how elaborate and careful the planning, all attempts at international dialogue end in more and more ludicrous failures. In the end, no one has any more faith in those who even attempt the dialogue. On the contrary, the negotiators, with all their pathetic good will, become the objects of contempt and of hatred. It is the "men of good will," the men who have made their poor efforts to do something about peace, who will in the end be the most mercilessly reviled, crushed, and destroyed as victims of the universal self-hate of man which they have unfortunately only increased by the failure of their good intentions.

Perhaps we still have a basically superstitious tendency to associate failure with dishonesty and guilt — failure being interpreted as "punishment." Even if a man starts out with good intentions, if he fails we tend to think he was somehow "at fault." If he was not guilty, he was at least "wrong." And "being wrong" is something we have not yet learned to face with equanimity and understanding. We either condemn it with god-like disdain or forgive it with god-like condescension. We do not manage to accept it with human compassion, humility, and identification. Thus we never see the one truth that would help us begin to solve our ethical and political problems: that we are *all* more or less wrong, and that we are *all* at fault, all limited and obstructed by our mixed motives, our self-deception, our greed, our self-righteousness, and our tendency to aggressivity and hypocrisy.

In our refusal to accept the partially good intentions of others and work with them (of course prudently and with resignation to the inevitable imperfection of the result) we are unconsciously proclaiming our own malice, our own intolerance, our own lack of realism, our own ethical and political quackery.

Perhaps in the end the first real step toward peace would be a realistic acceptance of the fact that our political ideals are perhaps to a great extent illusions and fictions to which we cling out of motives that are not always perfectly honest: that because of this we prevent ourselves from seeing any good or any practicability in the political ideas of our enemies — which may of course be in many ways even more illusory and dishonest than our own. We will never get anywhere unless we can accept the fact that politics is an inextricable tangle of good and evil motives in which, perhaps, the evil predominate but where one must continue to hope doggedly in what little good can still be found.

But someone will say: "If we once recognize that we are all equally wrong, all political action will instantly be paralyzed. We can only act when we assume that we are in the right." On the contrary, I believe the basis for valid political action can only be the recognition that the true solution to our problems is *not* accessible to any one isolated party or nation but that all must arrive at it by working together.

I do not mean to encourage the guilt-ridden thinking that is always too glad to be "wrong" in everything. This too is an evasion of responsibility, because every form of oversimplification tends to make decisions ultimately meaningless. We must try to accept ourselves whether individually or collectively, not only as perfectly good or perfectly bad, but in our mysterious, unaccountable mixture of good and evil. We have to stand by the modicum of good that is in us without exaggerating it. We have to defend our real rights, because unless we respect our own rights we will certainly not respect the rights of others. But at the same time we have to recognize that we have willfully or otherwise trespassed on the rights of others. We must be able to admit this not only as the result of self-examination, but when it is pointed out unexpectedly, and perhaps not too gently, by somebody else.

These principles which govern personal moral conduct, which make harmony possible in small social units like the family, also apply in the wider area of the state and in the whole community of nations. It is however quite absurd, in our present situation or in any other, to expect these principles to be universally accepted as the result of moral exhortations. There is very little hope that the world will be run according to them all of a sudden, as a result of some hypothetical change of heart on the part of politicians. It is useless and even laughable to base political thought on the faint hope of a purely contingent and subjective moral illumination in the hearts of the world's leaders. But outside of political thought and action, in the religious sphere, it is not only permissible to hope for such a mysterious consummation, but it is necessary to pray for it. We can and must believe not so much that the mysterious light of God can "convert" the ones who are mostly responsible for the world's peace, but at least that they may, in spite of their obstinacy and their prejudices, be guarded against fatal error.

It would be sentimental folly to expect men to trust one another when they obviously cannot be trusted. But at least they can learn to trust God. They can bring themselves to see that the mysterious power of God can, quite independently of human malice and error, protect men unaccountably against themselves, and that He can always turn evil into good, though perhaps not always in a sense that would be understood by the preachers of sunshine and uplift. If they can trust and love God, Who is infinitely wise and Who rules the lives of men, permitting them to use their freedom even to the point of almost incredible abuse, they can love men who are evil. They can learn to love them even in their sin, as God has loved them. If we can love the men we cannot trust (without trusting them foolishly) and if we can to some extent share the burden of their sin by identifying ourselves with them, then perhaps there is some hope of a kind of peace on earth, based not on the wisdom and the manipulations of men but on the inscrutable mercy of God.

For only love — which means humility — can exorcise the fear which is at the root of all war.

What is the use of postmarking our mail with exhortations to "pray for peace" and then spending billions of dollars on atomic submarines, thermonuclear weapons, and ballistic missiles? This, I would think, would certainly be what the New Testament calls "mocking God" — and mocking Him far more effectively than the atheists do. The culminating horror of the joke is that we are piling up these weapons to protect ourselves against atheists who, quite frankly, believe there is no God and are convinced that one has to rely on bombs and missiles since nothing else offers any real security. Is it then because we have so much trust in the power of God that we are intent upon utterly destroying these people before they can destroy us? Even at the risk of destroying ourselves at the same time?

I do not mean to imply that prayer excludes the simultaneous use of ordinary human means to accomplish a naturally good and justifiable end. One can very well pray for a restoration of physical health and at the same time take medicine prescribed by a doctor. In fact a believer should normally do both. And there would seem to be a reasonable and right proportion between the use of these two means to the same end.

But consider the utterly fabulous amount of money, planning, energy, anxiety, and care which go into the production of weapons which almost immediately become obsolete and have to be scrapped. Contrast all this with the pitiful little gesture: "pray for peace" piously canceling our four-cent stamps! Think, too, of the disproportion between our piety and the enormous act of murderous destruction which we at the same time countenance without compunction and without shame! It does not even seem to enter our minds that there might be some incongruity in praying to the God of peace, the God Who told us to love one another as He has loved us, who warned us that they who took the sword would perish by it, and at the same time planning to annihilate not thousands but millions of civilians and soldiers, men, women, and children without discrimination, even with the almost infallible certainty of inviting the same annihilation for ourselves.

It may make sense for a sick man to pray for health and then take medicine, but I fail to see any sense at all in his praying for health and then drinking poison.

When I pray for peace I pray to pacify not only the Russians and the Chinese but above all my own nation and myself. When I pray for peace I pray to be protected not only from the Reds but also from the folly and blindness of my own country. When I pray for peace, I pray not only that the enemies of my country may cease to want war, but above all that my own country will cease to do the things that make war inevitable. In other words, when I pray for peace I am not just praying that the Russians will give up without a struggle and let us have our own way. I am praying that both we and the Russians may somehow be restored to sanity and learn how to work out our problems, as best we can, together instead of preparing for global suicide.

I am fully aware that this sounds utterly sentimental, archaic, and out of tune with an age of science. But I would like to submit that pseudo-scientific thinking in politics and sociology have so far less than this to offer. One thing I would like to add in all fairness is that the atomic scientists themselves are quite often the ones most concerned about the ethics of the situation, and that they are among the few who dare to open their mouths from time to time and say something about it. But who on earth listens?

If men really wanted peace, they would sincerely ask God for it and He would give it to them. But why should He give the world a peace which it does not really desire? The peace the world pretends to desire is really no peace at all.

To some men peace merely means the liberty to exploit other people without fear of retaliation or interference. To others peace means the freedom to rob brothers without interruption. To still others it means the leisure to devour the goods of the earth without being compelled to interrupt their pleasures to feed those whom their greed is starving. And to practically everybody peace simply means the absence of any physical violence that might cast a shadow over lives devoted to the satisfaction of their animal appetites for comfort and pleasure.

Many men like these have asked God for what they thought was "peace" and wondered why their prayer was not answered. They could not understand that it actually *was* answered. God left them with what they desired, for their idea of peace was only another form of war. The "cold war" is simply the normal consequence of our corruption of peace based on a policy of "every man for himself" in ethics, economics, and political life. It is absurd to hope for a solid peace based on fictions and illusions!

So instead of loving what you think is peace, love other men and love God above all. And instead of hating the people you think are warmongers, hate the appetites and the disorder in your own soul, which are the causes of war. If you love peace, then hate injustice, hate tyranny, hate greed — but hate these things in *yourself*, not in another.

– Two –

Nuclear War and Christian Responsibility

Commonweal invited Merton to write an article on peace in a nuclear age for their Christmas 1961 issue. In October he sent the article to the censors. Opposed by one censor, it was eventually approved, but not in time for Christmas. It was not published until February 9, 1962. Merton felt its publication that week was providential, since it coincided with the General Strike for Peace held in New York City.

Rather quickly he learned that it was one thing to publish in the *Catholic Worker,* whose readers would most likely be sympathetic to his views, quite another to reach a readership of much more divergent views. On March 16 Merton wrote to Wilbur H. Ferry:

> The top brass in the American hierarchy is getting wind of my articles and is expressing displeasure. An editorial in the Washington *Catholic Standard* [March 9, 1962], evidently by a Bishop [Bishop Philip Hannan, auxiliary bishop of Washington, was then editor], takes very strong exception to the *Commonweal* article. [*Hidden Ground of Love,* 210]

Merton did learn, however, that one member of the American hierarchy had apparently read his article with approval. Cardinal Albert Meyer, archbishop of Chicago, issued a Lenten pastoral letter in 1962 in which he clearly borrowed sentences and phrases from the *Commonweal* article.

Apart from this welcome support from Cardinal Meyer, Merton was distressed by what he considered a misreading of his article. Yet, typical of him, there were self-recriminations. On February 4, 1962, with the *Commonweal* article about to be published, he wrote to John Tracy Ellis and expressed some misgivings about what he had written: "I may have given a wrong impression by some rather sweeping statements, and I have rewritten the article" (*Hidden Ground of Love,* 176). As a matter of fact, he actually rewrote this article four different times. There is one version, fairly close to the original, but toned down a bit, which — as far as I have been able to ascertain — was never published in Merton's lifetime (though it is included in Zahn's *The Non-Violent Alternative* [pp. 12–19] under the title: "Peace: Christian Duties and Perspectives").

A second rewriting of the *Commonweal* article, much expanded, appeared in a safer place, the *Catholic Worker.* It was so lengthy that it had to be published in two parts (one in the May issue, the other in June). As a title for this two-part article, Merton chose a sentence that occurs near the very end of the *Commonweal* article: "We Have to Make Ourselves Heard." This long article eventually grew into a book, *Peace in a Post-Christian*

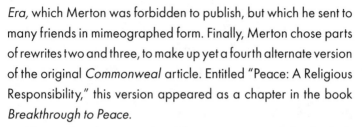
Era, which Merton was forbidden to publish, but which he sent to many friends in mimeographed form. Finally, Merton chose parts of rewrites two and three, to make up yet a fourth alternate version of the original *Commonweal* article. Entitled "Peace: A Religious Responsibility," this version appeared as a chapter in the book *Breakthrough to Peace.*

I have taken the time to detail the various stages through which this *Commonweal* article went to show its central importance in Merton's peace writing. These various rewrites also indicate something of the anguish, anxiety, and loneliness Merton experienced in presenting the positions he felt obliged to take.

It has been said so often that it has become a cliché, but it must be said again at the beginning of this article: the world and society of man now face destruction. *Possible* destruction: it is relatively easy, at the present time, to wipe out the entire human race either by nuclear, bacterial, or chemical agents, separately or together. *Probable* destruction: the possibility of destruction becomes a probability in proportion as the world's leaders commit themselves more and more irrevocably to policies built on the threat to use these agents of extermination. At the present moment, the United States and the Soviet bloc are committed to a policy of genocide. Not only are they committed to the use of nuclear weapons for self-defense, but even to their use in first-strike attack if it should be expedient. This means that the policies of the United States and Russia are now frankly built on the presumption that each one is able, willing, and *ready* to completely destroy the other at a moment's notice by a "first-strike"; that the one destroyed is capable of "post mortem retaliation" that would annihilate not only the attacker but all his allies and satellites, even though the defender were already wiped out himself.

There is no need to insist that in a world where another Hitler is very possible the mere existence of nuclear weapons constitutes the most tragic and serious problem that the human race has ever had to contend with. Indeed, the atmosphere of hatred, suspicion, and tension in which we all live is precisely what is needed to produce Hitlers.

It is no exaggeration to say that our times are Apocalyptic, in the sense that we seem to have come to a point at which all the hidden, mysterious dynamism of the "history of salvation" revealed in the Bible has flowered into final and decisive crisis. The term "end of the world" may or may not be one that we are capable of understanding. But at any rate we seem to be assisting in the unwrapping of the mysteriously vivid symbols of the last book of the New Testament. In their nakedness, they reveal to us our own selves as the men whose lot it is to live in the time of a possible ultimate decision.

We know that Christ came into this world as the Prince of Peace. We know that Christ Himself is our peace (Eph. 2:14). We believe that God has chosen for Himself, in the Mystical Body of Christ, an elect people, regenerated by the Blood of the Savior, and committed by their baptismal promise to wage war with the great enemy of peace and salvation. As Pope John XXIII pointed out in his first encyclical letter, *Ad Petri Cathedram,* Christians are obliged to strive for peace "with all the means at their disposal" and yet, as he continues, this peace cannot compromise with error or make concessions to it. Therefore it is by no means a matter of passive acquiescence in injustice, since this does not produce peace. However, the Christian struggle for peace depends first of all upon a free response of man to "God's call to the service of His merciful designs." The lack of man's response to this call, says Pope John, is the "most terrible problem of human history" (Christmas message, 1958). Christ our Lord did not come to bring peace to the world as a kind of spiritual tranquilizer. He brought to His disciples a vocation and a task, to struggle in the world of violence to establish His peace not only in their own hearts but in society itself.

The Christian is and must be by his very adoption as a son of God, in Christ, a peacemaker (Matt. 5:9). He is bound to imitate the Savior who, instead of defending Himself with twelve legions of Angels (Matt. 25:55) allowed Himself to be nailed *to the cross* and died praying for His executioners. The Christian is one whose life has sprung from a particular spiritual seed: the blood of the martyrs who, without offering forcible resistance, laid down their lives rather than submit to the unjust laws that demanded an official religious cult of the Emperor as God. That is to say, the Christian is bound, like the martyrs, to obey God rather than the state whenever the state tries to usurp powers that do not and cannot belong to it. We have repeatedly seen Christians in our time fulfilling this obligation in a heroic manner by their resistance to dictatorships that strove to interfere with the rights of their conscience and of their religion.

We are no longer living in a Christian world. The ages which we are pleased to call the "ages of Faith" were certainly not ages of earthly paradise. But at least our forefathers officially recognized and favored the Christian ethic of love. They fought some very bloody and un-Christian wars, and in doing so they also committed great crimes which remain in history as a permanent scandal. However, certain definite limits were recognized. Today a non-Christian world still retains a few vestiges of Christian morality, a few formulas and clichés, which serve on appropriate occasions to adorn indignant editorials and speeches. But otherwise we witness deliberate campaigns to eliminate all education in Christian truth and morality. The Christian ethic of love tends to be discredited as phony and sentimental.

It is therefore a serious error to imagine that because the West was once largely Christian, the cause of the Western nations is now to be identified, without further qualification, with the cause of God. The incentive to wipe out Bolshevism may well be one of the apocalyptic temptations of twentieth-century Christendom. It may indeed be the most effective way of destroying Christendom, even though man may survive. For who imagines that the Asians and Africans will respect Christianity and embrace it after it has apparently triggered mass-murder and destruction of cosmic proportions? It is pure madness to think that Christianity can defend itself with nuclear weapons. The mere fact that we now seem to accept nuclear war as reasonable is universal scandal.

True, Christianity is not only opposed to Communism, but is in a very real sense at war with it. This warfare, however, is spiritual and ideological. "Devoid of material weapons," says Pope John, "the Church is the trustee of the highest spiritual power." If the Church has no military weapons of her own, it means that her wars are fought without any weapons at all and not that she intends to call upon the weapons of nations that were once Christian.

We must remember that the Church does not belong to any political power bloc. Christianity exists on both sides of the Iron Curtain and we should feel ourselves united by very special bonds with those Christians who, living under Communism, often suffer heroically for their principles.

Is it a valid defense of Christianity for us to wipe out these heroic Christians along with their oppressors, for the sake of "religious freedom"? It is pure sophistry to claim that physical annihilation in nuclear war is a *"lesser evil"* than the difficult conditions under which these Christians continue to live, perhaps with true heroism and sanctity preserving their faith and witnessing very effectively to Christ in the midst of atheism. Persecution is certainly a physical evil and a spiritual danger, but Christ has said that those who suffer persecution in His Name are blessed (Matt. 5:10–12).

At the same time, one of the most disturbing things about the Western world of our times is that it is beginning to have much more in common with the communist world than it has with the professedly Christian society of several centuries ago. On both sides of the Iron Curtain we find two profoundly disturbing varieties of the same moral sickness: both of them rooted in the same fundamentally materialist view of life. Both are basically opportunistic and pragmatic in their own way. And both have the following characteristics in common. On the level of *morality* they are blindly passive in their submission to a determinism which, in effect, leaves men completely irresponsible. Therefore moral obligations and decisions have become practically meaningless. At best they are only forms of words, rationalizations of pragmatic decisions that have already been dictated by the needs of the moment.

Naturally, since not everyone is an unprincipled materialist even in Russia, there is bound to be some moral sense at work, even if only as a guilt-feeling that produces uneasiness and hesitation, blocking the smooth efficiency of machine-like obedience to immoral commands. Yet the history of Nazi Germany shows us how appalling was the irresponsibility which would carry on even the most revolting of crimes under cover of "obedience" for the sake of a "good cause." This moral passivity is the most terrible danger of our time, as the American Bishops have already pointed out in the joint letters of 1960 and 1961.

On the level of political, economic, and military activity, this moral passivity is balanced, or overbalanced, by a *demonic activism,* a frenzy of the most varied, versatile, complete, and even utterly brilliant technological improvisations, following one upon the other with an ever more bewildering and controllable proliferation. Politics pretends to use this force as its servant, to harness it for social purposes, for the "good of man." The intention is good. The technological development of power in our time is certainly a risk and challenge, but that does not make it intrinsically evil. On the contrary, it can and should be a very great good. In actual fact, however, the furious speed with which our technological world is plunging toward disaster is evidence that no one is any longer fully in control — and this includes the political leaders.

A simple study of the steps which led to the dropping of the first A-bomb at Hiroshima is devastating evidence of the way well-meaning men, the scientists and leaders of a victorious nation, were guided step by step, without realizing it, by the inscrutable yet simple "logic of events" to fire the shot that was to make the cold war inevitable and prepare the way perhaps inexorably for World War III. This they did purely and simply because they thought in all sincerity that the bomb was the simplest and most merciful way of ending World War II and perhaps all wars, forever.

The tragedy of our time is then not so much the malice of the wicked as the helpless futility even of the best intentions of "the good." There are warmakers, war criminals, indeed. They are present and active *on both sides*. But all of us, in our very best efforts for peace, find ourselves maneuvered unconsciously into positions where we too can act as war criminals. For there can be no doubt that

Hiroshima and Nagasaki were, though not fully deliberate crimes, nevertheless crimes. And who was responsible? No one. Or "history." We cannot go on playing with nuclear fire and shrugging off the results as "history." We are the ones concerned. We are the ones responsible. History does not make us, we make it — or end it.

In plain words, in order to save ourselves from destruction we have to try to regain control of a world that is speeding downhill without brakes, because of the combination of factors I have mentioned above: almost total passivity and irresponsibility on the moral level, plus the demonic activism in social, military, and political life. The remedy would seem to be to slow down our activity, especially all activity concerned with the production and testing of weapons of destruction, and indeed to backtrack by making every effort to negotiate for multilateral disarmament.

This may be of great help, but still only a palliative, not a solution. Yet *at least this* is perhaps feasible, and should at all costs be attempted, even at the cost of great sacrifice and greater risk. It is not morally licit for us as a nation to refuse the risk merely because our whole economy now depends on this war-effort. On the contrary, our national reliance on this substantial source of income and profit hardly qualifies as Christian.

Equally important, and perhaps even more difficult than disarmament, is the restoration of some moral sense and the resumption of genuine responsibility. Without this it is illusory for us to speak of freedom and "control." Unfortunately, even where moral principles are still regarded with some degree of respect, morality has lost touch with the realities of our situation. Moralists tend to discuss the problems of atomic war as if men still fought with bows and arrows. Modern warfare is fought as much by machines as by men. Even a great deal of the planning depends on the work of mechanical computers. An entirely new dimension is opened up by the fantastic process and techniques involved. An American President can speak of warfare in outer space and nobody bursts out laughing — he is perfectly serious. Science-fiction and the comic strips have all suddenly come true. When a missile armed with an H-bomb warhead is fired by the pressing of a button and its target is a whole city, the number of its victims is estimated in "megacorpses" — *millions* of dead human beings. A thousand or ten thousand more here and there are not even matter for comment. Under such conditions can there be serious meaning left in the fine decisions that were elaborated by scholastic theologians in the day of hand-to-hand combat? Can we assume that in atomic war the conditions which make double effect legitimate will be realized? Obviously not. And to make this perfectly clear, the explicit and formal declarations of governments leave no doubt that indiscriminate destruction is intended.

In atomic war, there is no longer the question of simply permitting an evil, the destruction of a few civilian dwellings, in order to attain a legitimate end: the destruction of a military target. It is well understood on both sides that atomic war is purely and simply massive and indiscriminate destruction of targets chosen not for their military significance alone, but for the importance in a calculated project of terror and annihilation. Often the selection of the target is determined by some quite secondary and accidental circumstance that has not the remotest reference to morality. Hiroshima was selected for atomic attack, among other reasons, because it had never undergone any noticeable air bombing and was suitable, as an intact target, to give a good idea of the effectiveness of the bomb.

It must be frankly admitted that some of the military commanders of both sides in World War II simply disregarded all traditional standards that were still effective. The Germans threw those standards overboard with the bombs they unloaded on Warsaw, Rotterdam, Coventry, and London. The allies replied in kind with the saturation bombing of Hamburg, Cologne, Dresden, and Berlin. Spokesmen were not wanting on either side, to justify these crimes against humanity. And today, while "experts" calmly discuss the possibility of the United States being able to survive a war if *"only fifty millions"* (!) of the population were killed; when the Chinese speak of being able to *"spare"* three hundred million and "still get along," it is obvious that we are no longer in the realm where moral truth is conceivable.

The only sane course that remains is to work frankly and without compromise for the total abolition of war. The pronouncements of the Holy See all point to this as the only ultimate solution. The first duty of the Christian is to help clarify thought on this point by taking the stand that all-out nuclear, bacterial, or chemical warfare is unacceptable as a practical solution to international problems because it would mean the destruction of the world. There is simply no "good end" that renders such a risk permissible or even thinkable on the level of ordinary common sense.

At this point someone will say, "The Church has not condemned nuclear war." First of all there is no need to condemn something that already quite obviously stands condemned by its very nature. Total war is murder. The fact that the Church tolerates limited war and even theoretically tolerates the limited use of "tactical" nuclear weapons for defensive purposes does not mean that she

either advocates or tolerates indiscriminate killing of civilians and military. Pope Pius XII, in 1954, made this
perfectly clear. He said: *"Should the evil consequences of
adopting this method of warfare ever become so exten-
sive as to pass entirely beyond the control of man, then
indeed its use must be rejected as immoral."* Uncontrolled
annihilation of human life is "not lawful under any title."
There is much debate over the term "entirely beyond control." If a missile with a nuclear warhead can be aimed
so as to destroy Leningrad rather than Helsinki, is this
sufficient to be termed control? One doubts this was the
mind of Pius XII.

It might be possible to get people to admit this in theory, but it is going to be very difficult in practice. They will
admit the theory because they will say that they "certainly
do not want a war" in which nuclear agents will be used
on an all-out scale. Obviously no one wants the destruction of the human race or of his own nation, although he
will not admit it in practice because foreign policy entirely
depends on wielding the threat of nuclear destruction. But
it is an issue of such desperate seriousness, we have to face
the fact that the calculated use of nuclear weapons as a
political threat is almost certain to lead eventually to a
hot war. Every time another hydrogen bomb is exploded
in a test, every time a political leader boasts his readiness
to use the same bomb on the cities of his enemy, we get

closer to the day when the missiles armed with nuclear warheads will start winging their way across the seas and the polar ice cap.

The danger must be faced. Whoever finds convenient excuses for this adventurous kind of policy, who rationalizes every decision dictated by political opportunism and justifies it, must stop to consider that he may be himself cooperating in the evil. On the contrary, our duty is to help emphasize with all the force at our disposal that the Church earnestly seeks the abolition of war; we must underscore declarations like those of Pope John XXIII pleading with world leaders to renounce force in the settlement of international disputes and confine themselves to negotiation.

Let us suppose that the political leaders of the world, supported by the mass media in their various countries, and carried onward by a tidal wave of even greater and greater war preparations, see themselves swept inexorably into a war of disastrous proportions. Let us suppose that it becomes morally certain that these leaders are helpless to arrest the blind force of the process that has been irresponsibly set in motion. What then? Are the masses of the world, including you and me, to resign themselves to their fate and march on to global suicide without resistance, simply bowing their heads and obeying their leaders as showing them the "will of God"? I think it should be evident to everyone that this can no longer, in the present situation, be accepted unequivocally as Christian obedience and civic duty.

On the contrary, this brings us face to face with the greatest and most agonizing moral issue of our time. This issue is not merely nuclear war, not merely the possible destruction of the human race by a sudden explosion of violence. It is something more subtle and more demonic. If we continue to yield to theoretically irresponsible determinism and to vague "historic forces" without striving to resist and to control them, if we let these forces drive us to demonic activism in the realm of politics and technology, we face something more than the material evil of universal destruction. We face *the moral responsibility of global suicide.* Much more than that, we are going to find ourselves gradually moving into a situation in which we are practically compelled by the "logic of circumstances" deliberately *to choose the course that leads to destruction.*

We all know the logic of temptation. We all know the vague, hesitant irresponsibility which leads us into the situation where it is no longer possible to turn back and how, arrived in that situation, we have a moment of clear-sighted desperation in which we freely commit ourselves to the course that we recognize to be evil. That may well be what is happening now to the whole world. The actual destruction of the human race is an enormous evil, but it is still, in itself, only a physical evil. Yet the free choice of global suicide, made in desperation by the world's leaders and ratified by the consent and cooperation of all their citizens, would be a moral evil second only to the crucifixion. The fact that such a choice might be made with the highest motives and the most urgent purpose would do nothing whatever to mitigate it. The fact that it might be made as a gamble, in the hope that some might escape, would never excuse it. After all, the purposes of Caiaphas were, in his own eyes, perfectly noble. He thought it was necessary to let "one man die for the people."

The most urgent necessity of our time is therefore not merely to prevent the destruction of the human race by nuclear war. Even if it should happen to be no longer possible to prevent the disaster (which God forbid), there is still a greater evil that can and must be prevented. It must be possible for every free man to refuse his consent and deny his cooperation to this greatest of crimes.

In what does this effective and manifest refusal of consent consist? How does one "resist" the sin of genocide? How are the conscientious objectors to mass suicide going to register their objection and their refusal to cooperate? Ideally speaking, in the imaginary case where all-out nuclear war seemed inevitable and the world's leaders seemed morally incapable of preventing it, it would become legitimate and even obligatory for all sane and conscientious men everywhere in the world to lay down their weapons and their tools and starve and be shot rather than cooperate in the war effort. If such a mass movement should spontaneously arise in all parts of the world, in Russia and America, in China and France, in Africa and Germany, the human race could be saved from extinction. This is indeed an engaging hypothesis — but it is no more than that. It would be folly to suppose that men hitherto passive, inert, morally indifferent, and irresponsible might suddenly recover their sense of obligation and their awareness of their own power when the world was on the very brink of war. Indeed we have already reached that point. Who says "No!" except for a few isolated individuals regarded almost generally as crackpots by everybody else?

It is vitally necessary that we form our conscience in regard to our own participation in the effort that threatens to lead us to universal destruction. We have to be convinced that there are certain things already clearly forbidden to all men, such as the use of torture, the killing of hostages, genocide (or the mass extermination of racial, national, or other groups for no reason other than that they belong to an "undesirable" category). The destruction of civilian centers by nuclear annihilation bombing is genocide. We have to become aware of the poisonous effect of the mass media that keep violence, cruelty and sadism constantly present in the minds of uninformed and irresponsible people. We have to recognize the danger to the whole world in the fact that today the economic life of the more highly developed nations is centered largely on the production of weapons, missiles, and other engines of destruction. We have to consider that hate propaganda, and the consistent nagging and baiting of one government by another, has always inevitably led to violent conflict. We have to recognize the implications of voting for politicians who promote policies of hate.

These are activities which, in view of their possible consequences, are so dangerous and absurd as to be morally intolerable. If we cooperate in these activities we share in the guilt they incur before God. It is no longer reasonable or right to leave all decisions to a largely anonymous power elite that is driving us all, in our passivity, toward ruin. We have to make ourselves heard. Christians have a grave responsibility to protest clearly and forcibly against trends that lead inevitably to crimes which the Church deplores and condemns. Ambiguity, hesitation, and compromise are no longer permissible. War must be abolished. A world government must be established. We have still time to do something about it, but the time is rapidly running out.

PART TWO

Following
the Year of the
Cold War Letters

Three

Danish Nonviolent Resistance to Hitler

Thomas Merton wrote this article under the pseudonym of Benedict Moore. It was published in the *Catholic Worker,* July–August 1963.

One of the rare glimmers of humanity in Eichmann's patient labors to exterminate the Jews, as recorded by Hannah Arendt's recent series of articles in the *New Yorker,* was the nonviolent resistance offered by the entire nation of Denmark against Nazi power mobilized for genocide.

Denmark was not the only European nation that disagreed with Hitler on this point. But it was one of the only nations which offered explicit, formal, and successful nonviolent resistance to Nazi power. The adjectives are important. The resistance was successful because it was explicit and formal, and because it was practically speaking unanimous. The entire Danish nation simply refused to cooperate with the Nazis and resisted every move of the Nazis against the Jews with nonviolent protest of the highest and most effective caliber, yet without any need for organization, training, or specialized activism: simply by unanimously and effectively expressing in word and action the force of their deeply held moral convictions. These moral convictions were nothing heroic or sublime. They were merely ordinary.

There had of course been subtle and covert refusals on the part of other nations. Italians in particular, while outwardly complying with Hitler's policy, often arranged to help the Jews evade capture or escape from unlocked freight cars. The Danish nation, from the King on down, formally and publicly rejected the policy and opposed it with an open, calm, convinced resistance which shook the morale of the German troops and SS men occupying the country and changed their whole outlook on the Jewish question.

When the Germans first approached the Danes about the segregation of Jews, proposing the introduction of the yellow badge, the government officials replied that the King of Denmark would be the first to wear the badge, and that the introduction of any anti-Jewish measures would lead immediately to their own resignation.

At the same time, the Danes refused to make any distinction between Danish and non-Danish Jews. That is to say, they took the German Jewish refugees under their protection and refused to deport them back to Germany — an act which considerably disrupted the efficiency of Eichmann's organization in Denmark until 1943 when Hitler personally ordered that the "final solution" go into effect without further postponement.

The Danes replied by strikes, by refusals to repair German ships in their shipyards, and by demonstrations of protest. The Germans then imposed martial law. But now it was realized that the German officials in Denmark were changed men. They could "no longer be trusted." They refused to cooperate in the liquidation of the Jews, not of course by open protest, but by delays, evasions, covert refusals, and the raising of bureaucratic obstacles. Hence Eichmann was forced to send a "specialist" to Denmark, at the same time making a concession of monumental proportions: all the Jews from Denmark would go only to Theresienstadt, a "soft" camp for privileged Jews. Finally, the special police sent direct from Germany to round up the Jews were warned by the SS officers in Denmark that Danish police would probably forcibly resist attempts to take the Jews away by force, and that there was to be no fighting between Germans and Danes. Meanwhile the Jews themselves had been warned and most of them had gone into hiding, helped of course by friendly Danes: then wealthy Danes put up money to pay for transportation of nearly six thousand Jews to Sweden, which offered them asylum, protection, and the right to work. Hundreds of Danes cooperated in ferrying Jews to Sweden in small boats. Half the Danish Jews remained safely in hiding in Denmark during the rest of the war. About five hundred Jews who were actually arrested in Denmark went to Theresienstadt and lived under comparatively good conditions: only forty-eight of them died, mostly of natural causes.

Denmark was certainly not the only European nation that disapproved more or less of the "solution" which Hitler had devised for the Judenfrage. But it was the only nation which, as a whole, expressed moral objection to this policy. Other nations kept their disapproval to themselves. They felt it was enough to offer the Jews "heartfelt sympathy," and, in many cases, tangible aid. But let us not forget that generally speaking the practice was to help the Jew at considerable profit to oneself. How many Jews in France, Holland, Hungary, etc., paid fortunes for official permits, bribes, transportation, protection, and still did not escape!

The whole Eichmann story, as told by Hannah Arendt (indeed as told by anybody) acquires a quality of hallucinatory awfulness from the way in which we see how people in many ways exactly like ourselves, claiming as we do to be Christians or at least to live by humanistic standards which approximate, in theory, to the Christian ethic, were able to rationalize a conscious, uninterrupted, and complete cooperation in activities which we now see to have been not only criminal but diabolical. Most of the rationalizing probably boiled down to the usual half-truths: "What can we do? There is no other way out, it is a necessary evil. True, we recognize this kind of action to be in many ways 'unpleasant.' We hate to have to take measures like these: but then those at the top know best. It is for the common good. The individual conscience has to be overruled when the common good is at stake. Our duty is to obey. The responsibility for those measures rests on others... etc."

Curiously, the Danish exception, while relieving the otherwise unmitigated horror of the story, actually adds to the nightmarish and hallucinated effect of incredulousness one gets while reading it. After all, the Danes were not even running a special kind of nonviolent movement. They were simply acting according to the ordinary beliefs which everybody in Europe theoretically possessed, but which, for some reason, nobody acted on. Quite the contrary! Why did a course of action which worked so simply and so well in Denmark not occur to all the other so-called

Christian nations of the West just as simply and just as spontaneously?

Obviously there is no simple answer. It does not even necessarily follow that the Danes are men of greater faith or deeper piety than other Western Europeans. But perhaps it is true that these people had been less perverted and secularized by the emptiness and cynicism, the thoughtlessness, the crude egoism, and the rank amorality which have become characteristic of our world, even where we still see an apparent surface of Christianity. It is not so much that the Danes were Christians as that they were human. How many others were even that?

The Danes were able to do what they did because they were able to make decisions that were based on clear convictions about which they all agreed and which were in accord with the inner truth of man's own rational nature, as well as in accordance with the fundamental law of God in the Old Testament as well as in the Gospel: thou shalt love thy neighbor as thyself. The Danes were able to resist the cruel stupidity of Nazi anti-Semitism because this fundamental truth was important to them. And because they were willing, in unanimous and concerted action, to stake their lives on this truth. In a word, such action becomes possible where fundamental truths are taken seriously.

– Four –

A Devout Meditation in Memory of Adolf Eichmann

This essay was first published in *New Directions in Prose and Poetry* (New Directions Publishing Co.) in the 1964 issue. It was later published in *Ramparts,* October 1966 and, also in 1966, in *Raids on the Unspeakable.* In a letter to Cid Corman of September 5, 1966 (*see Courage for Truth,* 248), Merton links this essay with his poem "Chants to Be Used in Processions Around a Site with Furnaces," which, he says, "is a sort of mosaic of Eichmann's own double-talk about himself."

One of the most disturbing facts that came out in the Eichmann trial was that a psychiatrist examined him and pronounced him *perfectly sane.* I do not doubt it at all, and this is precisely why I find it disturbing. If all the Nazis had been psychotics, as some of their leaders probably were, their appalling cruelty would have been in some sense easier to understand. It is much worse to consider this calm, "well-balanced," unperturbed official, conscientiously going about his desk work, his administrative job in the great organization: which happened to be the supervision of mass murder. He was thoughtful, orderly, unimaginative. He had a profound respect for system, for law and order. He was obedient, loyal, a faithful officer of a great state. He served his government very well.

He was not bothered much by guilt. I have not heard that he developed any psychosomatic illnesses. Apparently he slept well. He had a good appetite, or so it seems. True, when he visited Auschwitz, the camp commandant, Hoess, in a spirit of sly deviltry, tried to tease the big boss and scare him with some of the sights. Eichmann was disturbed, yes. He was disturbed. Even Himmler had been disturbed, and had gone weak at the knees. Perhaps, in the same way, the general manager of a big steel mill might be disturbed if an accident took place while he happened to be somewhere in the plant. But of course what happened at Auschwitz was not an accident: just the routine unpleasantness of the daily task. One must shoulder the burden of daily monotonous work for the Fatherland. Yes, one must suffer discomfort and even nausea from unpleasant sights and sounds. It all comes under the heading of duty, self-sacrifice, and obedience. Eichmann was devoted to duty, and proud of his job.

The sanity of Eichmann is disturbing. We equate sanity with a sense of justice, with humaneness, with prudence, with the capacity to love and understand other people. We are relying on the sane people of the world to preserve it from barbarism, madness, destruction. And now it begins to dawn on us that it is precisely the *sane* ones who are the most dangerous.

It is the sane ones, the well-adapted ones, who can without qualms and without nausea aim the missiles and press the buttons that will initiate the great festival of destruction that they, *the sane ones,* have prepared. What makes us so sure, after all, that the danger comes from a psychotic getting into a position to fire the first shot in a nuclear war? Psychotics will be suspect. The sane ones will keep them far from the button. No one suspects the sane, and the sane one will have *perfectly good reasons,* logical, well-adapted reasons, for firing the shot. They will be obeying sane orders that have come sanely down the chain of command. And because of their sanity they will have no qualms at all. When the missiles take off, then *it will be no mistake.*

In other words, then, we can no longer assume that because a man is "sane" he is therefore in his "right mind." The whole concept of sanity in a society where spiritual values have lost their meaning is itself meaning- less. A man can be "sane" in the limited sense that he is not impeded by his disordered emotions from acting in a cool, orderly manner, according to the needs and dictates of the social situation in which he finds himself. He can be perfectly "adjusted." God knows, perhaps such people can be perfectly adjusted even in hell itself.

And so I ask myself: what is the meaning of a concept of sanity that excludes love, considers it irrelevant, and destroys our capacity to love other human beings, to respond to their needs and their sufferings, to recognize them also as persons, to apprehend their pain as one's own? Evidently this is not necessary for "sanity" at all. It is a religious notion, a spiritual notion, a Christian notion. What business have we to equate "sanity" with "Christianity"? None at all, obviously. The worst error is to imagine that a Christian must try to be "sane" like everybody else, and that we *belong* in our kind of *society*. That we must be "realistic" about it. We must develop a *sane* Christianity: and there have been plenty of sane Christians in the past. Torture is nothing new, is it? We ought to be able to rationalize a little bit of brainwashing, and genocide, and find a place for nuclear war in our moral theology. Certainly some of us are doing our best along those lines already. There are hopes! Even Christians can shake off their sentimental prejudices about charity and become sane like Eichmann. They can even cling to a certain set of Christian formulas, and fit them into a Totalist

Ideology. Let them talk about justice, charity, love, and the rest. These words have not stopped some sane men from acting very sanely and cleverly in the past....

No, Eichmann was sane. The generals and fighters on both sides, in World War II, the ones who carried out the total destruction of entire cities, these were the sane ones. The ones who have invented and developed atomic bombs, thermonuclear bombs, missiles, who have planned the strategy of the next war; who have evaluated the various possibilities of using bacterial and chemical agents: these are not the crazy people, they are the *sane* people. The ones who coolly estimate how many millions of victims can be considered expendable in a nuclear war, I presume they do all right with the Rorschach ink blots too. On the other hand, you will probably find that the pacifists and the ban-the-bomb people are, quite seriously, just as we read in *Time,* a little crazy.

I am beginning to realize that "sanity" is no longer a value or an end in itself. The "sanity" of modern man is about as useful to him as the huge bulk and muscles of the dinosaur. If he were a little less sane, a little more doubtful, a little more aware of his absurdities and contradictions, perhaps there might be a possibility of his survival. But if he is sane, too sane ... or perhaps we must say that in a society like ours the worst insanity is to be totally without anxiety, totally "sane."

– Five –

Gandhi

The Gentle Revolutionary

Merton's interest in Gandhi goes back to his school days at Oakham School (as he mentions in this article). He studied Gandhi's writings and wrote two articles on him. The one became the introduction to a book of selected readings from Gandhi, appearing in the January 1965 issue of *Jubilee* under the title "Gandhi and the One-eyed Giant." The second article is the one that follows, which became part of *Seeds of Destruction* under the title of "A Tribute to Gandhi." Under the different title used here, Merton had sent it in April 1964 to Edward Keating, editor of *Ramparts*. "Does this piece on Gandhi," he asked, "strike you as something that would fit in with the nonviolence issue?" He adds quickly, "I have yet to consult the censors about it. It seems to me that this ought to be cleared, though I can never guarantee anything these days." The article was published in *Ramparts* in December 1964.

In 1931 Gandhi, who had been released from prison a few months before, came to London for a conference. The campaign of civil disobedience which had begun with the Salt March had recently ended. Now there were to be negotiations. He walked through the autumn fogs of London in clothes that were good for the tropics, not for England. He lived in the slums of London, coming from there to more noble buildings in which he conferred with statesmen. The English smiled at his bald head, his naked brown legs, the thin underpinnings of an old man who ate very little, who prayed. This was Asia, wise, disconcerting, in many ways unlovely, but determined upon some inscrutable project and probably very holy. Yet was it practical for statesmen to have conferences with a man reputed to be holy? What was the meaning of the fact that one could be holy, and fast, and pray, and be in jail, and be opposed to England all at the same time?

Gandhi thus confronted the England of the depression as a small, disquieting question mark. Everybody knew him, and many jokes were made about him. He was also respected. But respect implied neither agreement nor comprehension. It indicated nothing except that the man had gained public attention, and this was regarded as an achievement. Then, as now, no one particularly bothered to ask if the achievement signified something.

Yet I remember arguing about Gandhi in my school dormitory: chiefly against the football captain, the head prefect, who had come to turn out the flickering gaslight, and who stood with one hand in his pocket and a frown on his face which was not illuminated with understanding. I insisted that Gandhi was right, that India was, with perfect justice, demanding that the British withdraw peacefully and go home; that the millions of people who lived in India had a perfect right to run their own country. Such sentiments were of course beyond comprehension. How could Gandhi be right when he was *odd*? And how could I be right if I was on the side of someone who had the wrong kind of skin, and left altogether too much of it exposed?

A counterargument was offered but it was not an argument. It was a basic and sweeping assumption that the people of India were political and moral infants, incapable of taking care of themselves, backward people, primitive, uncivilized, benighted pagans, who could not survive without the English to do their thinking and planning for them. The British Raj was, in fact, a purely benevolent, civilizing enterprise for which the Indians were not suitably grateful....

Infuriated at the complacent idiocy of this argument, I tried to sleep and failed.

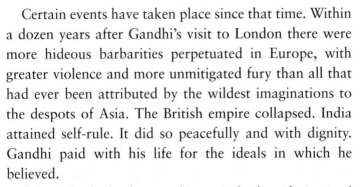

Certain events have taken place since that time. Within a dozen years after Gandhi's visit to London there were more hideous barbarities perpetuated in Europe, with greater violence and more unmitigated fury than all that had ever been attributed by the wildest imaginations to the despots of Asia. The British empire collapsed. India attained self-rule. It did so peacefully and with dignity. Gandhi paid with his life for the ideals in which he believed.

As one looks back over this period of confusion and decline in the West, the cold war, and the chaos and struggle of the world that was once colonial, there is one political figure who stands out from all the rest as an extraordinary leader of men. He is radically different from the others. Not that the others did not on occasion bear witness to the tradition of which they were proud because it was Christian. They were often respectable, sometimes virtuous men, and many of them were sincerely devout. Others were at least genteel. Others, of course, were criminals. Judging by their speeches, their programs, their expressed motives, they were civilized. Yet the best that could be said of them may be that they sometimes combined genuine capability and subjective honesty. But apart from that they seemed to be the powerless victims of a social dynamic that they were able neither to control nor to understand. They never seemed to dominate events, only to rush breathlessly after the parade of cataclysms, explaining why these had happened, and not aware of how they themselves had helped precipitate the worst of disasters. Thus with all their good intentions, they were able at best to rescue themselves after plunging blindly in directions quite other than those in which they claimed to be going. In the name of peace, they wrought enormous violence and destruction. In the name of liberty they exploited and enslaved. In the name of man they engaged in genocide or tolerated it. In the name of truth they systematically falsified and perverted truth.

Gandhi on the other hand was dedicated to peace, and though he was engaged in a bitter struggle for national liberation, he achieved this by peaceful means. He believed in serving the truth *by nonviolence,* and his *nonviolence* was effective insofar as it began first within himself, as obedience to the deepest truth in himself.

It is certainly true that Gandhi is not above all criticism, no man is. But it is evident that he was unlike all the other world leaders of his time in that his life was marked by a wholeness and a wisdom, an integrity and a spiritual consistency that the others lacked, or manifested only in reverse, in consistent fidelity to a dynamism of evil and destruction. There may be limitations in Gandhi's thought, and his work has not borne all the fruit he himself would have hoped. These are factors which he himself sagely took into account, and having reckoned with them all, he continued to pursue the course he had chosen simply because he believed it to be true. His way was no secret: it was simply to follow conscience without regard for the consequences to himself, in the belief that this was demanded of him by God and that the results would be the work of God. Perhaps indeed for a long time these results would remain hidden as God's secret. But in the end the truth would manifest itself.

What has Gandhi to do with Christianity? Everyone knows that the Orient has venerated Christ and distrusted Christians since the first colonizers and missionaries came from the West.

Western Christians often assume without much examination that this oriental respect for Christ is simply a vague, syncretistic, and perhaps romantic evasion of the challenge of the Gospel: an attempt to absorb the Christian message into the confusion and inertia which are thought to be characteristic of Asia. The point does not need to be argued here. Gandhi certainly spoke often of Jesus, whom he had learned to know through Tolstoy. And Gandhi knew the New Testament thoroughly. Whether or not Gandhi "believed in" Jesus in the sense that he had genuine faith in the Gospel would be very difficult to demonstrate, and it is not my business to prove it or disprove it. I think that the effort to do so would be irrelevant in any case. What is certainly true is that Gandhi not only understood the ethic of the Gospel, as well as, if not in some ways better, than most Christians, but he is one of the very few men of our time who applied Gospel principles to the problems of a political and social existence in such a way that his approach to these problems was *inseparably* religious and political at the same time.

He did this not because he thought that these principles were novel and interesting, or because they seemed expedient, or because of a compulsive need to feel spiritually secure. The religious basis of Gandhi's political action was not simply a program, in which politics were marshaled into the service of faith, and brought to bear on the charitable objectives of a religious institution. For Gandhi, strange as it may seem to us, political action had to be by its very nature "religious" in the sense that it had to be informed by principles of religious and philosophical wisdom. To separate religion and politics was in Gandhi's eyes "madness" because his politics rested on a thoroughly religious interpretation of reality, of life, and of man's place in the world. Gandhi's whole concept of man's relation to his own inner being and to the world of objects around him was informed by the contemplative heritage of Hinduism, together with the principles of Karma Yoga which blended, in his thought, with the ethic

78

of the Synoptic Gospels and the Sermon on the Mount. In such a view, politics had to be understood in the context of service and worship in the ancient sense of *leitourgia* (liturgy, public work). Man's intervention in the active life of society was at the same time by its very nature *svadharma,* his own personal service (of God and man) and worship, *yajna.* Political action therefore was not a means to acquire security and strength for one's self and one's party, but a means of witnessing to the truth and the reality of the cosmic structure by making one's own proper contribution to the order willed by God. One could thus preserve one's integrity and peace, being detached from results (which are in the hands of God) and being free from the inner violence that comes from division and untruth, the usurpation of someone else's *dharma* in place of one's own *svadharma.* These perspectives lent Gandhi's politics their extraordinary spiritual force and religious realism.

The success with which Gandhi applied this spiritual force to political action makes him uniquely important in our age. More than that, it gives him a very special importance for Christians. Our attitude to politics tends to be abstract, divisive, and often highly ambiguous. Political action is by definition secular and unspiritual. It has no really religious significance. We look to the Church to clarify principle and offer guidance, and in addition to that we are grateful if a Christian party of some sort comes to implement the program that has thus been outlined for us. This is all well and good. But Gandhi emphasized the importance of the individual person entering political action with a fully awakened and operative spiritual power in himself, the power of Satyagraha, nonviolent dedication to truth, a religious and spiritual force, a wisdom born of fasting and prayer. This is the charismatic and personal force of the saints, and we must admit that we have tended to regard it with mistrust and unbelief, as though it were mere "enthusiasm" and "fanaticism." This is a lamentable mistake, because for one thing it tends to short circuit the power and light of grace, and it suggests that spiritual dedication is and must remain something entirely divorced from political action: something for the *prie dieu,* the sacristy, or the study, but not for the marketplace. This in turn has estranged from the Church those whose idealism and generosity might have inspired a dedicated and creative intervention in political life. These have found refuge in groups dominated by a confused pseudo-spirituality, or by totalitarian messianism. Gandhi remains in our time as a sign of the genuine union of spiritual fervor and social action in the midst of a hundred pseudo-spiritual, cryptofascist, or communist movements in which the capacity for creative and spontaneous dedication is captured, debased, and exploited by the false prophets.

In a time when the unprincipled fabrication of lies and systematic violation of agreement has become a matter of course in power politics, Gandhi made this unconditional devotion to truth the mainspring of his social action. Once again, the radical difference between him and other leaders, even the most sincere and honest of them, becomes evident by the fact that Gandhi is chiefly concerned with truth and with service, *svadharma,* rather than with the possible success of his tactics upon other people, and paradoxically it was his religious conviction that made Gandhi a great politician rather than a mere tactician or operator. Note that *Satyagraha* is matter for a vow, therefore of worship, adoration of the God of truth, so that his whole political structure is built on this and his other vows (*Ahimsa,* etc.) and becomes an entirely religious system. The vow of *Satyagraha* is the vow to die rather than say what one does not mean.

The profound significance of *Satyagraha* becomes apparent when one reflects that "truth" here implies much more than simply conforming one's words to one's inner thought. It is not by words only that we speak. Our aims, our plans of action, our outlook, our attitudes, our habitual response to the problems and challenges of life, "speak" of our inner being and reveal our fidelity or infidelity to God and to ourselves. Our very existence, our life itself contains an implicit pretension to meaning, since all our free acts are implicit commitments, selections of "meanings" which we seem to find confronting us. Our very existence is "speech" interpreting reality. But the crisis of truth in the modern world comes from the bewildering complexity of the almost infinite contradictory propositions and claims to meaning uttered by millions of acts, movements, changes, decisions, attitudes, gestures, events, going on all around us. Most of all a crisis of truth is precipitated when men realize that almost all these claims to meaning and value are in fact without significance, when they are not in great part entirely fraudulent.

The tragedy of modern society lies partly in the fact that it is condemned to utter an infinite proliferation of statements when it has nothing to reveal except its own meaningless, its dishonesty, its moral indigence, its inner divisions, its abject spiritual void, its radical and self-destructive spirit of violence.

Satyagraha for Gandhi meant first of all refusing to say "nonviolence" and "peace" when one meant "violence" and "destruction." However, his wisdom differed from ours in this: he knew that in order to speak truth he must rectify more than his inner *intention*. It was not enough to say "love" and *intend* love thereafter proving the sincerity of one's own intentions by demonstrating the insincerity of one's adversary. "Meaning" is not a mental and subjective adjustment. For Gandhi, a whole lifetime of sacrifice was barely enough to demonstrate the sincerity with which he made a few simple claims: that he was not lying, that he did not *intend* to use violence or deceit against the English, that he did not think that peace and justice could be attained through violent or selfish means, that he did genuinely believe they could be assured by nonviolence and self-sacrifice.

Gandhi's religio-political action was based on an ancient metaphysics of man, a philosophical wisdom which is common to Hinduism, Buddhism, Islam, Judaism, and Christianity: that "truth is the inner law of our being." Not that man is merely an abstract essence, and that our action must be based on logical fidelity to a certain definition of man. Gandhi's religious action is based on a religious intuition of *being* in man and in the world, and his vow of truth is a vow of fidelity to being in all its accessible dimensions. His wisdom is based on experience more than on logic. Hence the way of peace is the way of truth, of fidelity to wholeness and being, which implies a basic respect for life not as a concept, not as a sentimental figment of the imagination, but its deepest, most secret and most frontal reality. The first and fundamental trust is to be sought in respect for our own inmost being, and this in turn implies the recollectedness and the awareness which attune us to that silence in which a lone Being speaks to us in all its simplicity.

Therefore Gandhi, recognized as no other world leader of our time, has done the necessity to be free from the pressures, the exorbitant and tyrannical demands of a society that is violent because it is essentially greedy, lustful and cruel. Therefore he fasted, observed days of silence, lived frequently in retreat, knew the value of solitude, as well as of the totally generous expenditure of his time and energy in listening to others and communicating with them. He recognized the impossibility of being a peaceful and nonviolent man if one submits passively to the insatiable requirements of a society maddened by overstimulation and obsessed with the demons of noise, voyeurism, and speed.

"Jesus died in vain," said Gandhi, "if he did not teach us to regulate the whole life by the eternal law of love." Strange that he should use this expression. It seems to imply at once concern and accusation. As Asians sometimes do, Gandhi did not hesitate to confront Christendom with the principles of Christ. Not that he judged Christianity, but he suggested that the professedly Christian civilization of the West was in fact judging itself by its own acts and its own fruits. There are certain Christian and humanitarian elements in Democracy, and if they are absent, Democracy finds itself on trial, weighed in the balance, and no amount of verbal protestations can prevent it from being found wanting. Events themselves will proceed inexorably to their conclusion. *Pacem in Terris* has suggested the same themes to the meditation of modern Europe, America and Russia. "Civilization" must learn to prove its claims by a capacity for the peaceful and honest settlement of disputes, by genuine concern for justice toward people who have been shamelessly exploited and races that have been systematically oppressed, or the historical preeminence of the existing powers will be snatched from them by violence, perhaps in a disaster of cosmic proportions.

Gandhi believed that the central problem of our time was the acceptance or the rejection of a basic law of love and of truth which had been made known to the world in traditional religions and most clearly by Jesus Christ. Gandhi himself expressly and very clearly declared himself an adherent of this one law. His whole life, his political action, finally even his death, were nothing but a witness to his commitment. "IF LOVE IS NOT THE LAW OF OUR BEING THE WHOLE OF MY ARGUMENT FALLS TO PIECES."

What remains to be said? It is true that Gandhi expressly dissociated himself from Christianity in its visible and institutional forms. But it is also true that he built his whole life and all his activity upon what he conceived to be the law of Christ. In fact, he died for this law which was at the heart of his belief. Gandhi was indisputably sincere and right in his moral commitment to the law of love and truth. A Christian can do nothing greater than follow his own conscience with a fidelity comparable to that with which Gandhi obeyed what he believed to be the voice of God. Gandhi is, it seems to me, a model of integrity whom we cannot afford to ignore, and the one basic duty we all owe to the world of our time is to imitate him in "dissociating ourselves from evil in total disregard of the consequences." May God mercifully grant us the grace to be half as sincere and half as generous as was this great leader, one of the noblest men of our century.

Six

Blessed Are the Meek

The Christian Roots of Nonviolence

On December 7, 1965, Merton received a letter from Hildegard Goss-Mayr asking him to write an article on "Demut" (Humility) for the journal *Der Christ in der Welt*. He agreed to do so and on January 14, 1966, he was able to write her that the article was completed: "It is the feast of St. Hilary, who said: 'The best way to solve the problem of rendering to Caesar what is Caesar's is to have nothing that is Caesar's.' This is a good day then to send you the essay on 'Demut,' which turned out to be really an essay on the beatitude of the Meek, as applied to Christian nonviolence" (*The Hidden Ground of Love*, 337). The article, translated into German, was published in the April–June 1965 issue of *Der Christ in der Welt*. It was published in English in the May 1967 issue of *Fellowship*. The Catholic Peace Fellowship issued it in July of that same year as a twelve-page pamphlet with a colorful cover designed by Sister Mary Corita. The pamphlet was dedicated to Joan Baez.

It would be a serious mistake to regard Christian non-violence simply as a novel tactic which is at once efficacious and even edifying, and which enables the sensitive man to participate in the struggles of the world without being dirtied with blood. Nonviolence is not simply a way of proving one's point and getting what one wants without being involved in behavior that one considers ugly and evil. Nor is it, for that matter, a means which anyone legitimately can make use of according to his fancy for any purpose whatever. To practice nonviolence for a purely selfish or arbitrary end would in fact discredit and distort the truth of nonviolent resistance.

Nonviolence is perhaps the most exacting of all forms of struggle, not only because it demands first of all that one be ready to suffer evil and even face the threat of death without violent retaliation, but because it excludes mere transient self-interest from its considerations. In a very real sense, he who practices nonviolent resistance must commit himself not to the defense of his own interests or even those of a particular group: he must commit himself to the defense of objective truth and right and above all of *man.* His aim is then not simply to "prevail" or to prove that he is right and the adversary wrong, or to make the adversary give in and yield what is demanded of him.

Nor should the nonviolent resister be content to prove to *himself* that *he* is virtuous and right, and that *his* hands and heart are pure even though the adversary's may be evil and defiled. Still less should he seek for himself the psychological gratification of upsetting the adversary's conscience and perhaps driving him to an act of bad faith and refusal of the truth. We know that our unconscious motives may, at times, make our nonviolence a form of moral aggression and even a subtle provocation designed (without awareness) to bring out the evil we hope to find in the adversary, and thus to justify ourselves in our own eyes and in the eyes of "decent people." Wherever there is a high moral ideal there is an attendant risk of pharisaism, and nonviolence is no exception. The basis of pharisaism is division: on one hand this morally or socially privileged self and the elite to which it belongs. On the other hand, the "others," the wicked, the unenlightened, whoever they may be, Communists, capitalists, colonialists, traitors, international Jewry, racists, etc.

Christian nonviolence is not built on a presupposed division, but on the basic unity of man. It is not out for the conversion of the wicked to the ideas of the good, but for the healing and reconciliation of man with himself, man the person and man the human family.

The nonviolent resister is not fighting simply for "his" truth or for "his" pure conscience, or for the right that is on "his side." On the contrary, both his strength and his weakness come from the fact that he is fighting for *the* truth, common to him and to the adversary, *the* right which is objective and universal. He is fighting for *everybody.*

For this very reason, as Gandhi saw, the fully consistent practice of nonviolence demands a solid metaphysical and religious basis both in being and in God. This comes *before* subjective good intentions and sincerity. For the Hindu this metaphysical basis was provided by the Vedantist doctrine of the Atman, the true transcendent Self which alone is absolutely real, and before which the empirical self of the individual must be effaced in the faithful practice of *dharma.* For the Christian, the basis of nonviolence is the Gospel message of salvation *for all men* and of the Kingdom of God to which *all* are summoned. The disciple of Christ, he who has heard the good news, the announcement of the Lord's coming and of His victory, and is aware of the definitive establishment of the Kingdom, proves his faith by the gift of his whole self to the Lord in order that *all* may enter the Kingdom. This Christian discipleship entails a certain way of acting, a *politeia,* a *conservatio,* which is proper to the Kingdom.

The great historical event, the coming of the Kingdom, is made clear and is "realized" in proportion as Christians themselves live the life of the Kingdom in the circumstances of their own place and time. The saving grace of God in the Lord Jesus is proclaimed to man existentially in the love, the openness, the simplicity, the humility, and the self-sacrifice of Christians. By their example of a truly Christian understanding of the world, expressed in a living and active application of the Christian faith to the human problems of their own time, Christians manifest the love of Christ for men (John 13:35, 17:21), and by that fact make him visibly present in the world. The religious basis of Christian nonviolence is then faith in Christ the Redeemer and obedience to his demand to love and manifest himself in us by a certain manner of acting in the world and in relation to other men. This obedience enables us to live as true citizens of the Kingdom, in which the divine mercy, the grace, favor, and redeeming love of God are active in our lives. Then the Holy Spirit will indeed "rest upon us" and act in us, not for our own good alone but for God and his Kingdom. And if the Spirit dwells in us and works in us, our lives will be continuous and progressive conversion and transformation in which we also, in some measure, help to transform others and allow ourselves to be transformed by and with others in Christ.

The chief place in which this new mode of life is set forth in detail is the Sermon on the Mount. At the very beginning of this great inaugural discourse, the Lord numbers the beatitudes, which are the theological foundation of Christian nonviolence: Blessed are the poor in spirit . . . blessed are the meek (Matt. 5:3–4).

This does not mean "blessed are they who are endowed with a tranquil natural temperament, who are not easily moved to anger, who are always quiet and obedient, who do not naturally resist." Still less does it mean "blessed are they who passively submit to unjust oppression." On the contrary, we know that the "poor in spirit" are those of whom the prophets spoke, those who in the last days will be the "humble of the earth," that is to say the oppressed who have no human weapons to rely on and who nevertheless are true to the commandments of Yahweh, and who hear the voice that tells them: "Seek justice, seek humility, perhaps you will find shelter on the day of the Lord's wrath" (Zeph. 2:3). In other words they seek justice in the power of truth and of God, not by the power of man. Note that Christian meekness, which is essential to true nonviolence, has this eschatological quality about it. It refrains from self-assertion and from violent aggression because it sees all things in the light of the great judgment. Hence it does not struggle and fight merely for this or that ephemeral gain. It struggles for the truth and the right which alone will stand in that day when all is to be tried by fire (1 Cor. 3:10–15).

Furthermore, Christian nonviolence and meekness imply a particular understanding of the power of human poverty and powerlessness when they are united with the invisible strength of Christ. The beatitudes indeed convey a profound existential understanding of the dynamic of the Kingdom of God — a dynamic made clear in the parables of the mustard seed and of the yeast. This is a dynamism of patient and secret growth, in belief that out of the smallest, weakest, and most insignificant seed the greatest tree will come. This is not merely a matter of blind and arbitrary faith. The early history of the Church, the record of the apostles and martyrs remains to testify to this inherent and mysterious dynamism of the ecclesial "event" in the world of history and time. Christian nonviolence is rooted in this consciousness and this faith.

This aspect of Christian nonviolence is extremely important and it gives us the key to a proper understanding of the meekness which accepts being "without strength" (*gewaltlos*) not out of masochism, quietism, defeatism, or false passivity, but trusting in the strength of the Lord of truth. Indeed, we repeat, Christian nonviolence is nothing if not first of all a formal profession of faith in the Gospel message that *the Kingdom has been established* and that the Lord of truth is indeed risen and reigning over his Kingdom.

Faith of course tells us that we live in a time of eschato-logical struggle, facing a fierce combat which marshals all the forces of evil and darkness against the still-invisible truth, yet this combat is already decided by the vic-tory of Christ over death and over sin. The Christian can renounce the protection of violence and risk being humble, therefore *vulnerable,* not because he trusts in the supposed efficacy of a gentle and persuasive tactic that will disarm hatred and tame cruelty, but because he believes that the hidden power of the Gospel is demand-ing to be manifested in and through his own poor person. Hence in perfect obedience to the Gospel, he effaces him-self and his own interests and even risks his life in order to testify not simply to "the truth" in a sweeping, idealistic and purely platonic sense, but to the truth that is incarnate in a concrete human situation, involving living persons whose rights are denied or whose lives are threatened.

Here it must be remarked that a holy zeal for the cause of humanity in the abstract may sometimes be mere love-lessness and indifference for concrete and living human beings. When we appeal to the highest and most noble ideals, we are most easily tempted to hate and condemn those who, so we believe, are standing in the way of their realization.

Christian nonviolence does not encourage or excuse hatred of a special class, nation, or social group. It is not merely *anti-* this or that. In other words, the evangelical realism which is demanded of the Christian should make it impossible for him to generalize about "the wicked" against whom he takes up moral arms in a struggle for righteousness. He will not let himself be persuaded that the adversary is totally wicked and can therefore never be reasonable or well-intentioned, and hence need be listened to. This attitude, which defeats the very purpose of nonviolence — openness, communication, dialogue — often accounts for the fact that some acts of civil disobedience merely antagonize the adversary without making him willing to communicate in any way whatever, except with bullets or missiles. Thomas à Becket, in Eliot's play *Murder in the Cathedral,* debated with himself, fearing that he might be seeking martyrdom merely in order to demonstrate his own righteousness and the King's injustice: "This is the greatest treason, to do the right thing for the wrong reason."

Now all these principles are fine and they accord with our Christian faith. But once we view the principles in the light of current *facts,* a practical difficulty confronts us. If the "gospel is preached to the poor," if the Christian message is essentially a message of hope and redemption for the poor, the oppressed, the underprivileged, and those who have no power humanly speaking, how are we to reconcile ourselves to the fact that Christians belong for the most part to the rich and powerful nations of the earth. Seventeen percent of the world's population control eighty percent of the world's wealth, and most of these seventeen percent are supposedly Christian. Admittedly those Christians who are interested in nonviolence are not ordinarily the wealthy ones. Nevertheless, like it or not, they share in the power and privilege of the most wealthy and mighty society the world has ever known. Even with the best subjective intentions in the world, how can they avoid a certain ambiguity in preaching nonviolence? Is this not a mystification?

We must remember Marx's accusation that "the social principles of Christianity encourage dullness, lack of self-respect, submissiveness, self-abasement, in short all the characteristics of the proletariat." We must frankly face the possibility that the nonviolence of the European or American preaching Christian meekness may conceivably be adulterated by bourgeois feelings and by an unconscious desire to preserve the status quo against violent upheaval.

On the other hand, Marx's view of Christianity is obviously tendentious and distorted. A real understanding of Christian nonviolence (backed up by the evidence of history in the Apostolic Age) shows not only that it is a *power*, but that it remains perhaps the only really effective way of transforming man and human society. After nearly fifty years of Communist revolution, we find little evidence that the world is improved by violence. Let us however seriously consider at least the *conditions* for relative honesty in the practice of Christian nonviolence.

1. Nonviolence must be aimed above all at the transformation of the present state of the world, and it must therefore be free from all occult, unconscious connivance with an unjust use of power. This poses enormous problems — for if nonviolence is too political it becomes drawn into the power struggle and identified with one side or another in that struggle, while if it is totally apolitical it runs the risk of being ineffective or at best merely symbolic.

2. The nonviolent resistance of the Christian who belongs to one of the powerful nations and who is himself in some sense a privileged member of world society will have to be clearly not for *himself* but *for others*, that is for the poor and underprivileged. (Obviously in the case of Negroes in the United States, though they may be citizens of a privileged nation, their case is different. They are clearly entitled to wage a nonviolent struggle for their rights, but even for them this struggle should be primarily *for truth itself* — this being the source of their power.)

3. In the case of nonviolent struggle for peace — the threat of nuclear war abolishes all privileges. Under the bomb there is not much distinction between rich and

poor. In fact the richest nations are usually the most threatened. Nonviolence must simply avoid the ambiguity of an unclear and *confusing protest* that hardens the warmakers in their self-righteous blindness. This means in fact that *in this case above all nonviolence must avoid a facile and fanatical self-righteousness,* and refrain from being satisfied with dramatic self-justifying gestures.

4. Perhaps the most insidious temptation to be avoided is one which is characteristic of the power structure itself: this fetishism of immediate visible results. Modern society understands "possibilities" and "results" in terms of a superficial and quantitative idea of efficacy. One of the missions of Christian nonviolence is to restore a different standard of practical judgment in social conflicts. This means that the Christian humility of nonviolent action must establish itself in the minds and memories of modern man not only as *conceivable* and *possible,* but as a *desirable alternative* to what he now considers the only realistic possibility: namely political technique backed by force. Here the human dignity of nonviolence must manifest itself clearly in terms of a freedom and a nobility which are able to resist political manipulation and brute force and show them up as arbitrary, barbarous and irrational. This will not be easy. The temptation to get publicity and quick results by spectacular tricks or by forms of protest that are merely odd and provocative

but whose human meaning is not clear may defeat this purpose.

The realism of nonviolence must be made evident by humility and self-restraint which clearly show frankness and open-mindedness and invite the adversary to serious and reasonable discussion.

Instead of trying to use the adversary as leverage for one's own effort to realize an ideal, nonviolence seeks only to enter into a dialogue with him in order to attain, together with him, the common good of man. Nonviolence must be realistic and concrete. Like ordinary political action, it is no more than the "art of the possible." But precisely the advantage of nonviolence is that it has a *more Christian and more humane notion of what is possible.* Where the powerful believe that only power is efficacious, the nonviolent resister is persuaded of the superior efficacy of love, openness, peaceful negotiation, and above all of truth. For power can guarantee the interests of *some men* but it can never foster the good of *man.* Power always protects the good of some at the expense of all the others. Only love can attain and preserve the good of all. Any claim to build the security of *all* on force is a manifest imposture.

It is here that genuine humility is of the greatest importance. Such humility, united with true Christian courage (because it is based on trust in God and not in one's own ingenuity and tenacity), is itself a way of communicating the message that one is interested only in truth and in the genuine rights of others. Conversely, our authentic interest in the common good above all will help us to be humble, and to distrust our own hidden drive to self-assertion.

5. Christian nonviolence, therefore, is convinced that the manner in which the conflict for truth is waged will itself manifest or obscure the truth. To fight for truth by dishonest, violent, inhuman, or unreasonable means would simply betray the truth one is trying to vindicate. The absolute refusal of evil or suspect means is a necessary element in the witness of nonviolence.

As Pope Paul said before the United Nations Assembly in 1965, "Men cannot be brothers if they are not humble. No matter how justified it may appear, pride provokes tensions and struggles for prestige, domination, colonialism and egoism. In a word *pride shatters brotherhood.*" He went on to say that the attempts to establish peace on the basis of violence were in fact a manifestation of human pride. "If you wish to be brothers, let the weapons fall from your hands. You cannot love with offensive weapons in your hands."

6. A test of our sincerity in the practice of nonviolence is this: are we willing to *learn something from the adversary?* If a *new truth* is made known to us by him or

through him, will we accept it? Are we willing to admit
that he is not totally inhumane, wrong, unreasonable,
cruel, etc.? This is important. If he sees that we are completely incapable of listening to him with an open mind,
our nonviolence will have nothing to say to him except
that we distrust him and seek to outwit him. Our readiness to see some good in him and to agree with some of
his ideas (though tactically this might look like a weakness on our part), actually gives us power: the power of
sincerity and of truth. On the other hand, if we are obviously unwilling to accept any truth that we have not first
discovered and declared ourselves, we show by that very
fact that we are interested not in the truth so much as in
"being right." Since the adversary is presumably interested in being right also, and in proving himself right
by what he considers the superior argument of force, we
end up where we started. Nonviolence has great power,
provided that it really witnesses to truth and not just to
self-righteousness.

The dread of being open to the ideas of others generally comes from our hidden insecurity about our own
convictions. We fear that we may be "converted" — or
perverted — by a pernicious doctrine. On the other hand,
if we are mature and objective in our open-mindedness,
we may find that viewing things from a basically different
perspective — that of our adversary — we discover our

own truth in a new light and are able to understand our own ideal more realistically.

Our willingness to take *an alternative approach* to a problem will perhaps relax the obsessive fixation of the adversary on his view, which he believes is the only reasonable possibility and which he is determined to impose on everyone else by coercion.

It is refusal of alternatives — a compulsive state of mind which one might call the "ultimate complex" — which makes wars in order to force the unconditional acceptance of one oversimplified interpretation of reality. This mission of Christian humility in social life is not merely to edify, but to *keep minds open to many alternatives*. The rigidity of a certain type of Christian thought has seriously impaired this capacity, which nonviolence must recover.

Needless to say, Christian humility must not be confused with a mere desire to win approval and to find reassurance by conciliating others superficially.

7. Christian hope and Christian humility are inseparable. The quality of nonviolence is decided largely by the purity of the Christian hope behind it. In its insistence on certain human values, the Second Vatican Council, following *Pacem in Terris*, displayed a basically optimistic trust *in man himself*. Not that there is not wickedness in the world, but today trust in God cannot be completely divorced from a certain trust in man. The Christian knows

102

that there are radically sound possibilities in every man, and he believes that love and grace always have the power to bring out those possibilities at the most unexpected moments. Therefore if he has hopes that God will grant peace to the world it is because he also trusts that man, God's creature, is not basically evil: that there is in man a potentiality for peace and order which can be realized provided the right conditions are there. The Christian will do his part in creating these conditions by preferring love and trust to hate and suspiciousness. Obviously, once again, this "hope in man" must not be naive. But experience itself has shown, in the last few years, how much an attitude of simplicity and openness can do to break down barriers of suspicion that had divided men for centuries.

It is therefore very important to understand that Christian humility implies not only a certain wise reserve in regard to one's own judgments — a good sense which sees that we are not always necessarily infallible in our ideas — but it also cherishes positive and trustful expectations of others. A supposed "humility" which is simply depressed about itself and about the world is usually a false humility. This negative, self-pitying "humility" may cling desperately to dark and apocalyptic expectations and refuse to let go of them. It is secretly convinced that only tragedy and evil can possibly come from our present world situation. This secret conviction cannot be kept hidden. It will manifest itself in our attitudes, in our social action, and in our protest. It will show that in fact we despair of reasonable dialogue with anyone. It will show that we expect only the worst. Our action seeks only to block or frustrate the adversary in some way. A protest that from the start declares itself to be in despair is hardly likely to have valuable results. At best it provides an outlet for the personal frustrations of the one protesting. It enables him to articulate his despair in public. This is not the function of Christian nonviolence. This pseudo-prophetic desperation has nothing to do with the beatitudes, even the third. No blessedness has been promised to those who are merely sorry for themselves.

In resume, the meekness and humility which Christ extolled in the Sermon on the Mount and which are the basis of true Christian nonviolence are inseparable from an eschatological Christian hope which is completely open to the presence of God in the world and therefore in the presence of our brother who is always seen, no matter who he may be, in the perspectives of the Kingdom. Despair is not permitted to the meek, the humble, the afflicted, the ones famished for justice, the merciful, the clean of heart and the peacemakers. All the beatitudes "hope against hope," "bear everything, believe everything, hope for everything, endure everything" (1 Cor.

13:7). The beatitudes are simply aspects of love. They refuse to despair of the world and abandon it to a supposedly evil fate which it has brought upon itself. Instead, like Christ himself, the Christian takes upon his own shoulders the yoke of the Savior, meek and humble of heart. This yoke is the burden of the world's sin with all its confusions and all its problems. These sins, confusions, and problems are our very own. We do not disown them.

Christian nonviolence derives its hope from the promise of Christ: "Fear not, little flock, for the Father has prepared for you a Kingdom" (Luke 12:32).

The hope of the Christian must be, like the hope of a child, pure and full of trust. The child is totally available in the present because he has relatively little to remember, his experience of evil is as yet brief, and his anticipation of the future does not extend far. The Christian, in his humility and faith, must be as totally available to his brother, to his world, in the present, as the child is. But he cannot see the world with childlike innocence and simplicity unless his memory is cleared of past evils by forgiveness, and his anticipation of the future is hopefully free of craft and calculation. For this reason, the humility of Christian nonviolence is at once patient and uncalculating. The chief difference between nonviolence and violence is that the latter depends entirely on its own calculations. The former depends entirely on God and on His word.

At the same time the violent or coercive approach to the solution of human problems considers man in general, in the abstract, and according to various notions about the laws that govern his nature. In other words, it is concerned with man as subject to necessity, and it seeks out the points at which his nature is consistently vulnerable in order to coerce him physically or psychologically. Nonviolence on the other hand is based on that respect for the human person without which there is no deep and genuine Christianity. It is concerned with an appeal to the liberty and intelligence of the person insofar as he is able to transcend nature and natural necessity. Instead of forcing a decision upon him from the outside, it invites him to arrive freely at a decision of his own, in dialogue and cooperation, and in the presence of that truth which Christian nonviolence brings into full view by its sacrificial witness. The key to nonviolence is the willingness of the nonviolent resister to suffer a certain amount of accidental evil in order to bring about a change of mind in the oppressor and awaken him to personal openness and to dialogue. A nonviolent protest that merely seeks to gain publicity and to show up the oppressor for what he is, without opening his eyes to new values, can be said to be in large part a failure. At the same time, a nonviolence which does not rise to the level of the personal and remains confined to the consideration of nature and natural necessity may perhaps make a deal but it cannot really make sense.

It is understandable that the Second Vatican Council, which placed such strong emphasis on the dignity of the human person and the freedom of the individual conscience, should also have strongly approved "those who renounce the use of violence in the vindication of their rights and who resort to methods of defense which are otherwise available to weaker parties too" (*Constitution on the Church in the Modern World,* no. 78). In such a confrontation between conflicting parties, on the level of personality, intelligence, and freedom, instead of with massive weapons or with trickery and deceit, a fully human solution becomes possible. Conflict will never be abolished but a new way of solving it can become habitual. Man can then act according to the dignity of that adulthood which he is now said to have reached — and which yet remains, perhaps to be conclusively proved. One of the ways in which it can, without doubt, be proved is precisely this: man's ability to settle conflicts by reason and arbitration instead of by slaughter and destruction.

The distinction suggested here, between two types of thought — one oriented to nature and necessity, the other to persona and freedom — calls for further study at another time. It seems to be helpful. The "nature-oriented" mind treats other human beings as objects to be manipulated in order to control the course of events and make the future for the whole human species conform to certain rather rigidly determined expectations. "Person-oriented" thinking does not lay down these draconian demands, does not seek so much to *control* as to *respond*, and to *awaken response*. It is not set on determining anyone or anything, and does not insistently demand that persons and events correspond to our own abstract ideal. All it seeks is the openness of free exchange in which reason and love have freedom of action. In such a situation the future will take care of itself. This is the truly Christian outlook. Needless to say that many otherwise serious and sincere Christians are unfortunately dominated by this "nature-thinking," which is basically legalistic and technical. They never rise to the level of authentic interpersonal relationships outside their own intimate circle. For them, even today, the idea of building peace on a foundation of war and coercion is not incongruous — it seems perfectly reasonable!

Seven

Nhat Hanh Is My Brother

On May 28, 1966, Nhat Hanh, the Vietnamese monk, poet, and peacemaker, visited Merton at Gethsemani in company with John Heidbrink, head of the Fellowship of Reconciliation. Merton was impressed by the visit and wrote the following tribute.

This is not a political statement. It has no "interested" motive, it seeks to provoke no immediate action "for" or "against" this or that side in the Vietnam war. It is on the contrary a human and personal statement and an anguished plea for the Vietnamese Buddhist monk Thich Nhat Hanh, who is my brother. He is more my brother than many who are nearer to me by race and nationality, because he and I see things exactly the same way. He and I deplore the war that is ravaging his country. We deplore it for exactly the same reasons: human reasons, reasons of sanity, justice, and love. We deplore the needless destruction, the fantastic and callous ravaging of human life, the rape of the culture and spirit of an exhausted people. It is surely evident that this carnage serves no purpose that can be discerned and indeed contradicts the alleged intentions of the mighty nation that has constituted itself the "defender" of the people it is destroying.

Certainly this statement cannot help being a plea for peace. But it is also a plea for my brother Nhat Hanh. He represents the least "political" of all the movements in Vietnam. He is not directly associated with the Buddhists who are trying to use political manipulation in order to save their country. He is by no means a communist. The Vietcong is deeply hostile to him. He refuses to be identified with the established government, which hates and distrusts him. He represents the young, the defenseless, the new ranks of youth who find themselves with every hand turned against them except those of the peasants and the poor, with whom they are working. Nhat Hanh speaks truly for the people of Vietnam, if there can be said to be a "people" left in Vietnam.

Nhat Hanh has left his country and come to us in order to present a picture which is not given us in our newspapers and magazines. He has been well received — and that speaks well for those who have received him. His visit to the United States has shown that we are a people who still desire the truth when we can find it and still decide in favor of *man* against the political machine when we get a fair chance to do so. But when Nhat Hanh goes home, what will happen to him? He is not in favor with the government, which has suppressed his writings. The Vietcong will view with disfavor his American contacts. To have pleaded for an end to the fighting will make him a traitor in the eyes of those who stand to gain personally as long as the war goes on, as long as their countrymen are being killed, as long as they can do business with our military. Nhat Hanh may be returning to imprisonment, torture, even death. We cannot let him go back to Saigon to be destroyed while we sit here, cherishing the warm humanitarian glow of good intentions and worthy sentiments about the ongoing war. We who have met and heard Nhat Hanh, or have read about him, must also raise our voices to demand that his life and freedom be respected when he returns to his country. Furthermore, we demand this not in terms of any conceivable political advantage, but purely in the name of those values of freedom and humanity in favor of which our armed forces declare they are fighting the Vietnam war.

Nhat Hanh is a free man who has acted as a free man in favor of his brothers and moved by the spiritual dynamic of a tradition of religious compassion. He has come among us as many others have, from time to time, bearing witness to the spirit of Zen. More than any other he has shown us that Zen is not an esoteric and world-denying cult of inner illumination, but that it has its rare

111

and unique sense of responsibility in the modern world. Wherever he goes he will walk in the strength of his spirit and in the solitude of the Zen monk who sees beyond life and death. It is for our own honor as much as for his safety that we must raise our voices to demand that his life and personal integrity be fully respected when he returns to his smashed and gutted country, there to continue his work with the students and peasants, hoping for the day when reconstruction can begin.

I have said Nhat Hanh is my brother, and it is true. We are both monks, and we have lived the monastic life about the same number of years. We are both poets, existentialists. I have far more in common with Nhat Hanh than I have with many Americans, and I do not hesitate to say it. It is vitally important that such bonds be admitted. They are the bonds of a new solidarity and a new brotherhood which is beginning to be evident on all the five continents and which cut across all political, religious, and cultural lines to unite young men and women in every country in something that is more concrete than an ideal and more alive than a program. This unity of the young is the only hope of the world. In its name I appeal for Nhat Hanh. Do what you can for him. If I mean something to you, then let me put it this way: do for Nhat Hanh whatever you would do for me if I were in his position. In many ways I wish I were.

– Eight –

Ishi

A Meditation

This article reviews Theodora Kroeber's book *Ishi in Two Worlds: A Biography of the Last Wild Indian in North America.* It is one of five essays by Merton published in 1976 by Unicorn Press in a book entitled *Ishi Means Man.* The article fits well with Merton's other writings on the struggles between whites and non-whites in American society. It was also published in the March 1967 issue of the *Catholic Worker.*

"Genocide" is a new word. Perhaps the word is new because technology has not got into the game of destroying whole races at once. The destruction of races is not new — just easier. Nor is it a speciality of totalitarian regimes. We have forgotten that a century ago white America was engaged in the destruction of entire tribes and ethnic groups of Indians. The trauma of California gold. And the vigilantes who, in spite of every plea from

Washington for restraint and understanding, repeatedly took matters into their own hands and went out slaughtering Indians. Indiscriminate destruction of the "good" along with the "bad" — just so long as they were Indians. Parties of riffraff from the mining camps and saloons suddenly constituted themselves defenders of civilization. They armed and went out to spill blood and gather scalps. They not only combed the woods and canyons — they even went into the bars and ranch houses, to find and destroy the Indian servants and hired people, in spite of the protests of the ranchers who employed them.

The Yana Indians (including the Yahi or Mill Creeks) lived around the foothills of Mount Lassen, east of the Sacramento River. Their country came within a few miles of Vina, where the Trappist monastery in California stands today. These hill tribes were less easy to subdue than their valley neighbors. More courageous and more aloof, they tried to keep clear of the white man altogether. They were not necessarily more ferocious than other Indians, but because they kept to themselves and had a legendary reputation as "fighters," they were more feared. They were understood to be completely "savage." As they were driven further and further back into the hills, and as their traditional hunting grounds gradually narrowed and emptied of game, they had to raid the ranches in order to keep alive. White reprisals were to be expected

114

and they were ruthless. The Indians defended themselves by guerrilla warfare. The whites decided that there could be no peaceful coexistence with such neighbors. The Yahi, or Mill Creek Indians, as they were called, were marked for complete destruction. Hence they were regarded as subhuman. Against them there were no restrictions and no rules. No treaties need be made, for no Indian could be trusted. Where was the point in "negotiation"?

Ishi, the last survivor of the Mill Creek Indians, whose story was published by the University of California at Berkeley three years ago (Theodora Kroeber, *Ishi in Two Worlds: A Biography of the Last Wild Indian in North America* [Berkeley and Los Angeles: University of California Press, 1961]), was born during the war of extermination against his people. The fact that the last Mill Creeks were able to go into hiding and to survive for another fifty years in their woods and canyons is extraordinary enough. But the courage, the resourcefulness, and the sheer nobility of these few stone-age men struggling to preserve their life, their autonomy, and their identity as a people rises to the level of tragic myth. Yet there is nothing mythical about it. The story is told with impeccable objectivity — though also with compassion — by the scholars who finally saved Ishi and learned from him his language, his culture, and his tribal history.

To read this story thoughtfully, to open one's ear to it, is to receive a most significant message: one that not only moves, but disturbs. You begin to feel the inner stirrings of that pity and dread which Aristotle said were the purifying effect of tragedy. "The history of Ishi and his people," says the author, Theodora Kroeber, "is inexorably part of our own history. We have absorbed their lands into our holdings. Just so must we be the responsible custodians of their tragedy, absorbing it into our tradition and morality." Unfortunately, we learned little or nothing about ourselves from the Indian wars!

"They have separated murder into two parts and fastened the worse on me" — words which William Carlos Williams put on the lips of a Viking exile, Eric the Red. Men are always separating murder into two parts: one which is unholy and unclean: for "the enemy." Another which is a sacred duty: "for our side." He who first makes the separation, in order that he may kill, proves his bad faith. So too in the Indian wars. Why do we always assume the Indian was the Aggressor? We were in *his* country, we were taking it over for ourselves, and we likewise refused even to share any with him. We were the people of God, always in the right, following a manifest destiny. The Indian could only be a devil. But once we allow ourselves to see all sides of the question, the familiar perspectives of American history undergo a change.

116

The "savages" suddenly become human and the "whites," the "civilized," can seem barbarians. True, the Indians were often cruel and inhumane (some more than others). True, also the humanity, the intelligence, the compassion and understanding which Ishi met with in his friends the scholars, when he came to join our civilization, restore the balance in our favor. But we are left with a deep sense of guilt and shame. The record is there. The Mill Creek Indians, who were once seen as bloodthirsty devils, were peaceful, innocent, and deeply wronged human beings. In their use of violence they were, so it seems, generally very fair. It is we who were the wanton murderers, and they who were the innocent victims. The loving kindness lavished on Ishi in the end did nothing to change that fact. His race had been barbarously, pointlessly destroyed.

The impact of the story is all the greater because the events are so deeply charged with a natural symbolism: the structure of these happenings is such that it leaves a haunting imprint on the mind. Out of that imprint come disturbing and potent reflections.

Take, for example, the scene in 1870 when the Mill Creeks were down to their last twenty or thirty survivors. A group had been captured. A delegation from the tiny remnant of the tribe appeared at a ranch to negotiate. In a symbolic gesture, they handed over five bows (five being a sacred number) and stood unarmed waiting for an answer. The gesture was not properly understood, though it was evident that the Indians were trying to recover their captives and promising to abandon all hostilities. In effect, the message was: "Leave us alone, in peace, in our hills, and we will not bother you any more. We are few, you are many, why destroy us? We are no longer any menace to you." No formal answer was given. While the Indians were waiting for some kind of intelligible response, one of the whites slung a rope over the branch of a tree. The Indians quietly withdrew into the woods.

From then on, for the next twelve years, the Yahi disappeared into the hills without a trace. There were perhaps twenty of them left, one of whom was Ishi, together with his mother and sister. In order to preserve their identity as a tribe, they had decided that there was no alternative but to keep completely away from white men, and have nothing whatever to do with them. Since coexistence was impossible, they would try to be as if they did not exist for the white man at all. To be there as if they were not there.

In fact, not a Yahi was seen. No campfire smoke rose over the trees. Not a trace of fire was found. No village was discovered. No track of an Indian was observed. The Yahi remnant (and that phrase takes on haunting biblical resonances) systematically learned to live as invisible and as unknown.

To anyone who has ever felt in himself the stirrings of a monastic or solitary vocation, the notion is stirring. It has implications that are simply beyond speech. There is nothing one can say in the presence of such a happening and of its connotations for what our spiritual books so glibly call "the hidden life." The "hidden life" is surely not irrelevant to our modern world: nor is it a life of spiritual comfort and tranquility which a chosen minority can happily enjoy, at the price of a funny costume and a few prayers. The "hidden life" is the extremely difficult life that is forced upon a remnant that has to stay completely out of sight in order to escape destruction.

This so-called long concealment of the Mill Creek Indians is not romanticized by any means. The account is sober, objective, though it cannot help being an admiring tribute to the extraordinary courage and ingenuity of these lost stone-age people. Let the book speak for itself.

The long concealment failed in its objective to save a people's life but it would seem to have been brilliantly successful in its psychology and techniques of living.... Ishi's group was a master of the difficult art of communal and peaceful coexistence in the presence of alarm and in a tragic and deteriorating prospect.... It is a curious circumstance that some of the questions which arise about the concealment,

119

are those for which in a different context psychologists and neurologists are trying to find answers for the submarine and outer space services today. Some of these are: what makes for morale under confining and limiting life-conditions? What are the presumable limits of claustrophobic endurance? It seems that the Yahi might have qualified for outer space had they lasted into this century.

There is something challenging and awe-inspiring about this thoughtful passage by a scientifically trained mind. And that phrase about "qualifying for outer space" has an eerie ring about it. Does someone pick up the half-heard suggestion that the man who wants to live a normal life span during the next two hundred years of our history must be the kind of person who is "qualified for outer space"? Let us return to Ishi! The following sentences are significant:

In contrast to the Forty-niners … whose morality and morale had crumbled, Ishi and his band remained incorrupt, humane, compassionate, and with their faith intact even unto starvation, pain and death. The questions then are: what makes for stability? For psychic strength? For endurance, courage, faith?

The answers given by the author to these questions are mere suggestions. The Yahi were on their own home ground. This idea is not developed. The reader should reflect a little on the relation of the Indian to the land on which he lived. In this sense, most modern men never know what it means to have a "home ground." Then there is a casual reference to the "American Indian mystique" which could also be developed. William Faulkner's hunting stories, particularly "The Bear," give us some idea of what his "mystique" might involve. The word "mystique" has unfortunate connotations: it suggests an emotional icing on an ideological cake. Actually the Indian lived by a deeply religious wisdom which can be called in a broad sense mystical, and that is certainly much more than "a mystique." The book does not go into religious questions very deeply, but it shows us Ishi as a man sustained by a deep and unassailable spiritual strength which he never discussed.

Later, when he was living "in civilization" and was something of a celebrity as well as an object of charitable concern, Ishi was questioned about religion by a well-meaning lady. Ishi's English was liable to be unpredictable, and the language of his reply was not without its own ironic depths of absurdity:

"Do you believe in God?" the lady inquired.
"Sure, Mike!" he retorted briskly.

There is something dreadfully eloquent about this innocent short-circuit in communication.

One other very important remark is made by the author. The Yahi found strength in the incontrovertible fact that they were in the right. "*Of very great importance to their psychic health was the circumstance that their suffering and curtailments arose from wrongs done in them by others.* They were not guilt-ridden."

Contrast this with the spectacle of our own country with its incomparable technological power, its unequaled material strength, and its psychic turmoil, its moral confusion and its profound heritage of guilt which neither the righteous declarations of Cardinals nor the moral indifference of "realists" can do anything to change! Every bomb we drop on a defenseless Asian village, every Asian child we disfigure or destroy with fire only adds to the moral strength of those we wish to destroy for our own profit. It does not make the Vietcong cause just; but by an accumulation of injustice done against innocent people we drive them into the arms of our enemies and make our own ideals look like the most pitiful sham.

Gradually the last members of the Yahi tribe died out. The situation of the survivors became more and more desperate. They could not continue to keep up their perfect invisibility: they had to steal food. Finally the hidden camp where Ishi lived with his sister and sick mother was discovered by surveyors who callously walked off with the few objects they found as souvenirs. The mother and sister died, and finally on August 29, 1911, Ishi surrendered to the white race, expecting to be destroyed.

Actually, the news of this "last wild Indian" reached the anthropology department at Berkeley and a professor quickly took charge of things. He came and got the "wild man" out of jail. Ishi spent the rest of his life in San Francisco patiently teaching his hitherto completely unknown (and quite sophisticated) language to experts like Sapir. Curiously enough, Ishi lived in an anthropological museum where he earned his living as a kind of caretaker and also functioned, on occasion, as a live exhibit. He was well treated, and in fact the affection and charm of his relations with his white friends are not the least moving part of his story. He adapted to life in the city without too much trouble and returned once, with his friends, to live several months in his old territory, under his natural conditions, showing them how the Yahi had carried out the fantastic operation of their invisible survival. But he finally succumbed to one of the diseases of civilization. He died of TB in 1916, after four and a half years among the white men.

For the reflective reader who is — as everyone must be today — deeply concerned about man and his fate, this is a moving and significant book, one of those unusually suggestive works that *must* be read, and perhaps more than once. It is a book to think deeply about and take notes on not only because of its extraordinary factual interest but because of its special quality as a kind of parable.

One cannot help thinking today of the Vietnam war in terms of the Indian wars of a hundred years ago. Here again, one meets the same myths and misunderstandings, the same obsession with "completely wiping out" an enemy regarded as diabolical. The language of the vigilantes had overtones of puritanism in it. The backwoods had to be "completely cleaned out," or "purified" of Indians — as if they were vermin. I have read accounts of American GIs taking the same attitude toward the Vietcong. The jungles are thought to be "infested" with Communists, and hence one goes after them as one would go after ants in the kitchen back home. And in this process of "cleaning up" (the language of "cleansing" appeases and pacifies the conscience) one becomes without realizing it a murderer of women and children. But this is an unfortunate accident, what the moralists call "double effect." Something that is just too bad, but which must be accepted in view of something more important that has to be done. And so there is more and more killing of civilians and less and less of the "something more important" which is what we are trying to achieve. In the end, it is the civilians that are killed in the ordinary course of events, and combatants only get killed by accident. No one worries any more about double effect. War is waged against the innocent to "break enemy morale."

What is most significant is that Vietnam seems to have become an extension of our old Western frontier, complete with enemies of another, "inferior" race. This is a real "new frontier" that enables us to continue the cowboys-and-Indians game which seems to be part and parcel of our national identity. What a pity that so many innocent people have to pay with their lives for our obsessive fantasies!

One last thing. Ishi never told anyone his real name. The California Indians apparently never uttered their own names, and were very careful about how they spoke the name of others. Ishi would never refer to the dead by name either. "He never revealed his own private Yahi name," says the author. "It was as though it had been consumed in the funeral pyre of the last of his loved ones."

In the end, no one ever found out a single name of the vanished community. Not even Ishi's. For Ishi means simply MAN.

– Nine –

Auschwitz

A Family Camp

This essay was a review of *Auschwitz: A Report on the Proceedings against Robert Karl Ludwig Mulka and Others before the Court of Frankfurt* by Bernd Naumann, translated from the German by Jean Steinberg, with an introduction by Hannah Arendt (London: Pall Mall Press, 1966). The essay was published in the *Catholic Worker*, November 1967.

On December 20, 1963, twenty-two former SS men who had played important parts in the "final solution of the Jewish question" at Auschwitz went on trial at Frankfurt. The trial lasted twenty months. Scores of survivors of the camp, together with many other witnesses, testified to the massive torture and butchery accomplished twenty years before, in that curious place "far away, somewhere in Poland." The testimony does not make pleasant reading. It fills a book, in large format running to nearly 450 pages:

and this is only a summary of the most important points. The defendants were convicted and sentenced to prison terms, which they have all appealed. The most curious thing about the trial is that the defendants confidently and consistently denied almost everything. Finally the judge remarked in astonishment that he had "yet to meet anyone who had done anything at Auschwitz"! There was, in other words, a marked contrast between the unanimity of the witnesses saying black and the unanimity of the defendants saying white. Still more curiously, these same defendants had previously admitted much more of the dark side of the picture themselves. But now this has been "forgotten." They have somehow changed their minds. Hannah Arendt, in an important introduction, interprets this to mean that the German public has tacitly come to terms with the grim past. It has now apparently accepted these men, and many others like them.

In spite of the general tone of outrage still noticeable on the level of the court and of the better newspapers, the defendants themselves remained contemptuous and at ease, certain of ultimate freedom and confident that they had the tacit approval of their peers. Keeping this in mind, we now turn to the book. We reflect on the workings of a death factory where some three or four million people were barbarously destroyed. Yet to judge by the testimony of these men who have been sentenced to prison for literally thousands of murders each, the camp was an innocent establishment, a place for "protective custody." It doubtless knew its moments of austerity, but on the whole, it was simply a camp where people went to be "reeducated." At times, it almost sounds like fairyland. . . .

Fairyland in Poland

Chief among the defendants was Robert Mulka. In July 1942, Mulka became deputy of the camp commandant, Hoess. Though second in command for about a year, he claimed to know nothing about the fact that many prisoners seemed to be dying and of course issued no orders that had any connection with these unfortunate occurrences. When questioned about his duties he said he had worried a lot about whether or not the camp could afford some entertainers he wished to bring there. He sometimes encountered death close at hand when he paraded at the honor funeral of one of the SS guards. Gas chambers? Yes, he had heard something about them over the camp grapevine. "Word," he said, "got out in the course of time." Crematory furnaces? He admitted having seen a red glow in the sky and wondered what it was: rumor had supplied details. When pressed to explain why he had not tried to discover the facts himself, he said there was "no one to ask." Not even Commandant Hoess? No, the commandant was an "opaque man." Were there no orders about the "special treatment" of "asocial elements" and the "disinfection" of undesirables? He admitted that "there were probably some general instructions" which of course bypassed his own department, for he was after all only second in command. Confronted with orders signed by himself he offered no explanation. At the end of the trial, when the prosecution was asking that Mulka be given life imprisonment for more than 36,500 murders, Mulka himself simply asked the court to consider "all the circumstances which at the time brought me into my conflict situation."

The other defendants all said the same. Even those who were accused of selecting the prisoners for extermination, of driving them into the gas chambers, naked, with dogs turned loose and tearing their flesh. Of beating them to death on the "Boger swing" in "rigorous interrogations." Of injecting phenol into their hearts and killing them. Of wiping them out in shootings that lasted two or three days. All these people were strangely unaware that Auschwitz had been an extermination camp and that they had been the exterminators. They admitted there were gas chambers "somewhere near the barracks" (And where were the barracks? "Somewhere near the gas chambers!"). Yes, sometimes one drove a truck up "near the barracks" and one became aware that "people were busy doing something." It was even observed that "some prisoners were lying around." Resting perhaps? Since resting was not the usual thing at Auschwitz, were they perhaps dead? Altogether hard to say. One had failed to notice.

What about "cap shooting"? Making the prisoners throw their caps away, ordering them to run over to pick up the caps, and then shooting them for "trying to escape"? What about genuine escape attempts (some of which even succeeded)? One of the former SS guards assured the court that there were no attempted escapes. Who would want to escape? Auschwitz, he said, was after all, "a family camp." Another of the defendants, when obligingly describing the camp layout, asked the court if it would like him to point out on the map the place where he had made "a children's playground with sandboxes for the little ones."

Yes, there were even little ones in Auschwitz. They were marked out for play.

"The children were playing ball," says a former prisoner, "and waiting unsuspectingly. . . . A woman guard came, and clapped her hands, and called out: 'All right now, let's stop. Now we take showers.' And then they ran down the steps into the room in which they undressed. And the guard took a little girl on her arm and carried her down. And the child pointed to the eagle emblem on

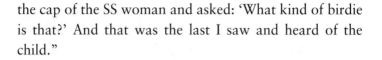

the cap of the SS woman and asked: 'What kind of birdie is that?' And that was the last I saw and heard of the child."

The Installations

No need to describe Auschwitz, the two huge death camps about three miles apart, the guard towers, the high barb-wire fences charged with thousands of volts, the barracks, the gas chambers, the furnaces burning day and night. The evil-smelling smoke. The glare in the night sky visible for miles. The ramp where the long freight trains arrived, the "transports" jammed with prisoners, men, women, children, from all parts of Europe. On the ramp, those selected for immediate gassing were told by a gesture to go to the right. Selection depended to some extent on the caprice or mood of the one in charge. But one could be "selected" in the camp itself. If a prisoner became seriously ill or too weak to work. If the barracks were getting too crowded. If conditions became inconvenient, efficiency might demand a housecleaning.

Delousings were not working properly in the women's camp. And a new doctor came along and solved the problem in a businesslike manner. "He simply had an entire block gassed." Having thus disposed of 750 women prisoners, he cleaned out the block, disinfected it, thoroughly deloused another batch of prisoners and moved them in. "He was the first to rid the entire women's camp of lice."

If Auschwitz was one of the main centers for the "final solution of the Jewish question" we must also remember it dealt with other problems too. Polish intellectuals and members of the Polish resistance were sent here for torture and liquidation. Thousands of Russian prisoners of war were exterminated at Auschwitz. According to the written testimony of one of the defendants (a deposition handed to the British at the end of the war) twelve thousand Russian prisoners of war reached Auschwitz early in 1942. In six months, there were only 150 of them still alive. "Thousands of prisoners of war were shot in a copse near Birkenau" (wrote the defendant Perry Broad). They were "buried in mass graves . . . the fisheries began to complain that the fish in the ponds in the vicinity of Birkenau were dying. Experts said this was due to the pollution of the ground water through cadaveric poison. . . . The summer sun was beating down on Birkenau, the bodies . . . started to swell up and a dark red mass started to seep through the cracks of the earth. . . . " This called for a quick and efficient solution, since the camp authorities did not like bad publicity. Twenty or thirty "very reliable SS men" were picked for the job. They had to sign a statement that if they violated their oath of secrecy or even hinted at the nature of their job they would be punished by death. This special detail then rounded up prisoners to do the digging. The prisoners chosen were Jews. The bodies of the Russians were exhumed and burned. "For weeks, thick white smoke continued to rise from that isolated tract of land." There were rumors. Prisoners who refused to do this job were shot. The others did not survive to tell about it. The SS men on this unpleasant detail were rewarded with "special rations from the SS kitchen: 1 quart of milk, sausages, cigarettes and of course liquor." This, it turned out, was standard practice and applied also to those who had the tiresome job of beating prisoners to death, or shooting them at the Black Wall, or putting them into the gas. When things were very busy an SS man, trying to show off his marksmanship, unfortunately shot a colleague. He was, of course, punished. One of the SS men, Klehr, was a male nurse — a "medical orderly." He specialized in injecting his patients in the heart with phenol and thus solving all their problems at once. He was also a notorious drunk, and was sometimes so intoxicated that he could no longer carry on the selections of appropriate candidates for the gas chamber. "Such selections had to be interrupted."

Klehr also had other hobbies. He was in charge of some rabbits: perhaps they were used for scientific experiments like the prisoners. At any rate he was so interested in the rabbits that he often "injected the prisoners two at a time because he wanted to get back to his rabbits." Such was the testimony of a former prisoner who had to hold the patients whom Klehr was injecting. One day the prisoner looked up and recognized the next patient in line. It was his father. Klehr was in a hurry and did not stop to ask why the prisoner was crying. He did so the next day, however. "Why," said Klehr in a burst of arbitrary generosity, "you should have told me. I would have let him live!" Favors were sometimes done at Auschwitz! The prisoner, however, had feared to speak, convinced that if he did so he would have got a shot of phenol in the heart himself.

The Children of Zamosc

Klehr took care of 120 Polish children from a village called Zamosc. They were killed in two batches: eighty the first day, the rest on the day after. Their parents were dead and no one quite knew what to do with them. They played in the courtyard of the hospital. "A ball had somehow turned up." Maybe that was when there were sandboxes. Another witness mentioned a balloon. But eventually the children were lined up and filed into the "examination room." Klehr was waiting for them with the syringe and the saucer of phenolic acid. The first ones screamed. After that it was somehow quieter. In the silence of the barrack, one heard the bodies falling off the chair and thumping onto the wooden floor. But Klehr did not do it all.

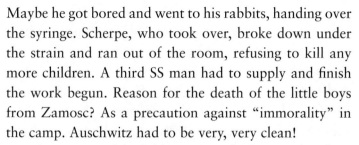

Maybe he got bored and went to his rabbits, handing over the syringe. Scherpe, who took over, broke down under the strain and ran out of the room, refusing to kill any more children. A third SS man had to supply and finish the work begun. Reason for the death of the little boys from Zamosc? As a precaution against "immorality" in the camp. Auschwitz had to be very, very clean!

Other scenes with children: Outside the gas chambers and crematories where mothers with children were sent immediately upon arrival. The mothers sometimes tried to hide the children under the piles of clothing. "Sometimes the voice of a little child who had been forgotten would emerge from beneath a pile of clothing.... They would put a bullet through its head."

Sometimes, children were not sent at once for "special treatment." They might be kept handy for medical experiments. In the interests of science! Or they might even be assigned to useful work. One witness who entered Auschwitz at fourteen and survived testified that he was on the cart detail that removed ashes from the crematory. "We got ashes from Crematory III and scattered them on the icy roads. When there were no people in the gas chambers, the capo let us warm ourselves there." Another less bucolic scene: an SS man who threw living children into the flames and boiling human fat of the open cremation pyres. And finally this, from a witness: "Early in

135

the morning I saw a little girl standing all by herself in the yard...wearing a claret-colored dress and [she had] a little pigtail. She held her hands at her side like a soldier. Once she looked down, wiped the dust off her shoes and again stood very still. Then I saw Boger come into the yard. He took the child by her hand — she went along very obediently — and stood her with her face to the Black Wall. Once she turned around. Boger again turned her head to the wall, walked back, and shot.... "

Exceptionally gentle for Boger, one of the most brutal professional butchers in the camp. He was sometimes seen to pick up little children by the heels and smash their heads against a brick wall.... But that was during a moment of stress in the mass liquidation of the Gypsy compound.

The Language of Auschwitz

Language itself has fallen victim to total war, genocide, and systematic tyranny in our time. In destroying human beings, and human values, on a mass scale, the Gestapo also subjected the German language to violence and crude perversion.

In Auschwitz secrecy was emphasized. "If you talk about what you can see from here," one prisoner was told, "you'll go through the chimney." Written records were kept cryptic, evasive. Great care was taken to destroy as much paperwork as possible before the Russians arrived. Even mention of corporal punishment was taboo. Any open reference to the realities of life and death in the camp was regarded as treason. Any guard, doctor, prison administrator who let out the truth could be severely punished for "defeatist talk."

This circumlocution was itself highly significant. It admitted the sinister and ironic fact that even knowledge of the truth about Auschwitz could furnish a formidable propaganda weapon to the enemies of the Reich. The very irony of the fact should have raised some urgent questions about the principle behind the camp. But the function of doubletalk and doublethink is to say everything without raising inconvenient questions. Officialese has a talent for discussing reality while denying it and calling truth itself into question. Yet the truth remains. This doubletalk is by its very nature invested with a curious metaphysical leer. The language of Auschwitz is one of the vulnerable spots through which we get a clear view of the demonic.

Gestapo doubletalk encircles reality as a doughnut encircles its hole. "Special treatment," "special housing." We need no more than one lesson, and we gain the intuition which identifies the hole, the void of death, in the heart of the expression. When the circumlocution becomes a little more insistent ("recovery camps for the tired") it brings with it suggestions of awful lassitude, infinite hopelessness, as if meaning had now been abolished forever and we were definitively at the mercy of the absurd.

"Disinfectants," "materials for resettlement of Jews," "ovaltine substitute from Swiss Red Cross" — all references to Zyklon B! When a deadly poison gas is referred to as soothing, restorative, a quasi-medicine to put babies to sleep, one senses behind the phrase a deep hatred of life itself. The key to Auschwitz language is its pathological joy in death. This turns out to be the key to all officialese. All of it is the celebration of boredom, of routine, of deadness, of organized futility. Auschwitz just carried the whole thing to its logical extreme, with a kind of heavy lilt in its mockery, its oafish love of death.

"Work makes free" — the sign over the gate of Auschwitz — tells, with grim satisfaction, the awful literal truth: "Here we work people to death." And behind it the dreadful metaphysical admission "For us there is only one freedom, death."

"To the Bath," said the sign pointing to the gas chambers. (You will be purified of that dirty thing, your life!) And as a matter of fact the gas chambers and crematories were kept spotlessly clean. "Nothing was left of them [the victims] not even a speck of dust on the armatures."

"Assigned to harvest duty" — this, in the record of an SS man, meant he had been posted to Auschwitz. The double meaning of "harvest" was doubtless not random. It has an apocalyptic ring.

Yet the Gestapo people had an acute sense of the importance of words. One of them became quite excited in court, over the distinction between "transferred" and "assigned."

Those who tortured escapees or resisters (and resistance could be expressed even by an expressionless face) praised the "Boger Swing" as their most effective language machine. The victim was hung from a horizontal pole, upside down, by wrists and ankles. He was whipped so vigorously that he often spun clean around on the pole. "You'll learn to talk, we have language for you," said the Gestapo men. "My talking machine will make you talk," said Boger, who was proud of his invention. In fact he has earned himself a place in history on account of it. Not an enviable place.

One of the results of the Frankfurt trial is that it makes an end of the pure Auschwitz myth: the myth of demented monsters who were twice our size, with six eyes and four rows of teeth, not of the same world as ourselves. The demonic sickness of Auschwitz emanated from ordinary people, stimulated by an extraordinary regime. The trial brought out their variety, their ordinariness, their shades of character, and even their capacity of change. In strict justice to Klehr, it must be said that he was profoundly affected by a visit from his wife in 1944, "a good kind woman . . . her two children were decent and well brought up." She did not suspect that her husband was involved in murder, but she knew that everything was not well at the camp. A witness overheard her saying to him, "I heard that terrible things happen here. I hope you're not involved." Klehr replied that he "cured people." But after his wife's visit, he began to treat prisoners more decently and to react against the camp methods. He even volunteered for front line duty, and when his request was refused, he denounced a brutal camp officer and had him transferred, thus improving conditions.

It is nevertheless eerie to read the testimony of a witness who had been a neighbor of the defendant Dr. Capesius in Bucharest, and met him on the ramp where he sent her sisters, brothers, and father to the gas chamber. "I still knew Dr. Capesius from Bucharest. . . . We lived in the same building. He was a representative of Bayer. Sometimes I spoke to him and his wife. . . . " The witness had even had coffee with Capesius and his wife in a park. That was the last time she saw him until 1944, at Auschwitz. "I recognized him right away . . . I was happy to see him. When I stood in front of him all he said was, 'How old are you?' and sent me to the right." However, it may be noted that in sending her to the right he had saved her life. Not even Boger can be regarded without qualification as a pure monster. Auschwitz becomes a little more horrible when we have to admit that Boger too is a human being.

Boger and his colleagues were all more or less the products of a society at least as respectable and as civilized as that of New York or London. They had all received an education, some of them higher education. They had been brought up, it is said, in "Christian homes," or at least in middle-class homes — not quite the same, but Christianity has been willing to overlook the possible differences. Before Hitler, they lived and moved among "respectable people" and since Hitler they have done the same. How is it that for twelve years in between they could beat and bash and torment and shoot and whip and murder thousands of their fellow human beings, *including even their former neighbors and friends,* and think nothing of it?

In the first place it would be wrong to say that they all thought nothing of it. One among the defendants who comes close to being tragic is Dr. Lucas. We sense in him a complex, lonely, tormented character who knew he was involved in a wrong that he could not entirely escape. Perhaps he might have escaped it. No one will ever be able to say with finality. But in any event he elected to go along with the system, to participate in the "selections," while at the same time practicing the ambivalent quasi-unconscious resistance technique of the "good soldier Schweik." Witness after witness spoke out in favor of Dr. Lucas. He was different from the others. Yes, he sent people to their death, but many witnesses recognized that he had saved their lives. Still he remained identified with the machinery of organized murder, and recognized that in so doing he had ruined his own life. Another who admitted that Auschwitz had been a doubtful quality in his life was Stark. He had gone to the camp as an SS guard when still in his teens. He had not yet finished school. Shooting, beating and killing were, for him, normal facts of life. He accepted them without question. He had practically grown up under Hitler and did not learn the difference until later. "I regret the mistakes of my past," he said, "but I cannot undo them."

What about Boger? Though he consistently denied everything said by witnesses, in the end his defense was content to ask for leniency rather than life imprisonment, on the grounds that Boger had merely done his duty as a good policeman.

This seems to sum up Boger's rather aggrieved view of his own case. Boger defended his "swing" right to the end. How could one refuse a conscientious police official the right to use "rigorous methods of interrogation"? Boger bluntly addressed the court on the virtues and necessity of these methods. They were highly practical. His defense lawyer expostulated with the jury: "The swing was not

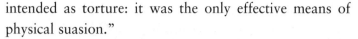
intended as torture: it was the only effective means of physical suasion."

The shocking thing about the views of both Boger and his lawyer is that they are evidently quite sincere. Not only that, they are views with which, it is assumed, other people will sympathize without difficulty.

In his final statement to the court, Boger made a distinction between the genocidal extermination of the Jews, which he admitted was perhaps a bit rough, and what he himself thought most important at the time: *"the fight against the Polish resistance movement and Bolshevism."*

Boger's case has now become an open appeal to the "good Germans" who, he assumes, agree with him; they will easily approve the rigors of his interrogation methods since they were justified by anti-Communism.

At this point, there swims into view a picture taken at another investigation (hardly a trial) in the state of Mississippi. We see the smiling, contemptuous, brutal faces of the police deputies and their colleagues who are allegedly the murderers of three civil rights workers in the summer of 1964. Whatever may have been the facts in the case, one feels that in Mississippi and Auschwitz the basic assumptions are not very different. Instead of seeing the Bogers and Klehrs of Auschwitz as fabulous, myth-sized and inhuman monsters, we come to recognize that people like them are in fact all around us. All they need is the right kind of crisis, and they will blossom out.

Salutary Reflections

Such is the first conclusion. We have learned to associate the incredible brutality and inhumanity of Auschwitz with ordinary respectable people, in an extraordinary situation.

Second: Auschwitz worked because these people wanted it to work. Instead of resisting it, rebelling against it, they put the best of their energies into making genocide a success. This was true not only of one or two psychopaths but of an entire bureaucratic officialdom, including not only the secret police and Nazi party members but also managers and employees of the industries which knowingly made use of the slave labor provided in such abundance by the camp.

Third: although it was usual to argue that "they had no choice" and that they were "forced" to comply with orders, the trial showed a more complex and less excusable picture of the defendants. Almost all of them committed gratuitous acts of arbitrary cruelty and violence which were forbidden even by the Gestapo's own rules. Some were even punished by the SS for these violations. Was there no choice? There are on record refusals of men who simply would not take part in murder and

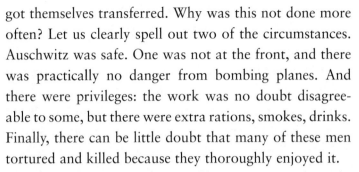

got themselves transferred. Why was this not done more often? Let us clearly spell out two of the circumstances. Auschwitz was safe. One was not at the front, and there was practically no danger from bombing planes. And there were privileges: the work was no doubt disagreeable to some, but there were extra rations, smokes, drinks. Finally, there can be little doubt that many of these men tortured and killed because they thoroughly enjoyed it.

Fourth: what does all this add up to? Given the right situation and another Hitler, places like Auschwitz can be set up, put into action, kept running smoothly, with thousands of people systematically starved, beaten, gassed, and whole crematories going full blast. Such camps can be set up tomorrow anywhere and made to work with the greatest efficiency, because there is no dearth of people who would be glad to do the job, provided it is sanctioned by authority. They will be glad because they will instinctively welcome and submit to an ideology which enables them to be violent and destructive without guilt. They are happy with a belief which turns them loose against their fellow man to destroy him cruelly and without compunction, as long as he belongs to a different race, or believes in a different set of semi-meaningless political slogans.

It is enough to affirm one basic principle: ANYONE BELONGING TO CLASS X OR NATION Y OR RACE Z IS TO BE

REGARDED AS SUBHUMAN AND WORTHLESS, AND CONSE-QUENTLY HAS NO RIGHT TO EXIST. All the rest will follow without difficulty.

As long as this principle is easily available, as long as it is taken for granted, as long as it can be spread out on the front pages at a moment's notice and accepted by all, we have no need of monsters: ordinary policemen and good citizens will take care of everything.

Ten

The Vietnam War

An Overwhelming Atrocity

This essay was published in the *Catholic Worker,* March 1968.

"No country may unjustly oppress others or unduly meddle in their affairs." (*Pacem in Terris,* no. 120)

"As men in their private enterprises cannot pursue their own interests to the detriment of others, so too states cannot lawfully seek the development of their own resources which brings harm to other states and unjustly oppresses them." (*Pacem in Terris,* no. 92)

In 1967 several young members of the International Volunteer Service in Vietnam resigned and returned to America, in protest against the way the war was, in their opinion, needlessly and hopelessly ravaging the country.

The International Volunteer Service is a nonprofit organization meant to help American youth to contribute to international goodwill by person-to-person contacts and service programs in other countries. Ambassador Lodge had called it "one of the success stories of American assistance," and obviously the men serving in Vietnam were in very close touch with the people, knew the language, and were perhaps better able to judge the state of affairs than most other Americans. As they said, they "dealt with people, not statistics," and they were in a position to know that the story of the Vietnam war is a very different one when it is learned from women and children whose flesh has been burned by napalm than it is when those same women and children appear in statistics as "enemy" casualties.

At this point, in case the reader is not fully aware of what napalm is, we might quote from a report of four American physicians on "Medical Problems of South Vietnam":

> Napalm is a highly sticky inflammable jelly which clings to anything it touches and burns with such heat that all oxygen in the area is exhausted within moments. Death is either by roasting or suffocation. Napalm wounds are often fatal (estimates are 90 percent). Those who survive face a living death. The victims are frequently children.

Another American physician wrote (Dr. R. E. Perry, *Redbook*, January 1967):

I have been an orthopedic surgeon for a good number of years with rather a wide range of medical experience. But nothing could have prepared me for my encounters with Vietnamese women and children burned by napalm. It was shocking and sickening even for a physician to see and smell the blackened and burned flesh.

By their resignation and by the statement they issued in an open letter to President Johnson, these men attempted to get through to the American public with a true idea of what the war really means to the Vietnamese — our allies, the ones we are supposedly "saving" from Communism. The attitude and feelings of the Vietnamese *people* (as distinct from the government) are too little known in the United States. They have been systematically ignored. Pictures of GI's bestowing candy bars upon half-naked "native" children are supposed to give us all the information we need in this regard. These are happy people who love our boys because we are saving them from the Reds and teaching them "democracy." It is of course important, psychologically and politically, for the public to believe this because otherwise the war itself would be questioned, and as a matter of fact it is questioned. Never was there a war in American history that was so much questioned! The official claim that such questioning is "betrayal" is a transparently gross and authoritarian attack on democratic liberty.

According to these Americans in the International Volunteer Service, men who cannot be considered leftists, still less as traitors, the American policy of victory at any price is simply destroying Vietnam. It is quite possible that the United States may eventually "win," but the price may be so high that there will be few left around to enjoy the fruits of victory and democracy in a country which we will, of course, obligingly reconstruct according to ideas of our own.

The people of South Vietnam have already had some experience of this kind of resettlement and reconstruction. Having seen their own homes burned or bulldozed out of existence, their fields and crops blasted with defoliants and herbicides, their livelihood and culture destroyed, they have been forcibly transplanted into places where they cannot live as they would like or as they know how, and forced into a society where, to adapt and be "at home" one has to be a hustler, a prostitute, or some kind of operator who knows how to get where the dollars are.

The people we are "liberating" in Vietnam are caught between two different kinds of terrorism, and the future presents them with nothing but a more and more bleak and hopeless prospect of unnatural and alienated existence. From their point of view, it doesn't matter much

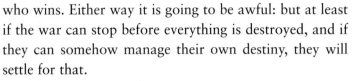

who wins. Either way it is going to be awful: but at least if the war can stop before everything is destroyed, and if they can somehow manage their own destiny, they will settle for that.

This, however, does not fit in with our ideas. We intend to go on bombing, burning, killing, bulldozing, and moving people around while the numbers of plague victims begin to mount sharply and while the "civilization" we have brought becomes more and more rotten. The people of South Vietnam believe that we are supporting a government of wealthy parasites they do not and cannot trust. They believe that the 1967 election was rigged, and they know that the two newspapers which protested about it were immediately silenced and closed down by the "democratic" government which we are supporting at such cost.

To put it plainly, according to the men who resigned from the International Volunteer Service, the people of South Vietnam are hardly grateful for "democracy" on such terms, and while they are quite willing to accept our dollars when they have a chance, they do not respect us or trust us. In point of fact, they have begun to hate us.

Far from weakening Communism in Asia by our war policy, we are only strengthening it. The Vietnamese are no lovers of China, but by the ruthlessness of our war for "total victory" we are driving them into the arms of the Red Chinese. "The war as it is now being waged," say the Volunteers, "is self-defeating." They support their contentions by quoting people they have known in Vietnam.

A youth leader: "When the Americans learn to respect the true aspirations in Vietnam, true nationalism will come to power. Only true nationalists can bring peace to the South, talk to the North and bring unification."

While a Catholic bishop in the United States was soothing President Johnson with the assurance the war in Vietnam is "a sad and heavy obligation imposed by the mandate of love," a Buddhist nun said in Vietnam: "You Americans come to help the Vietnamese people, but have brought only death and destruction. Most of us Vietnamese hate from the bottom of our hearts the Americans who have brought the suffering of this war...." After which she burned herself to death. That, too, was a drastic act of violence. Whether or not we may agree with it, we must admit that it lends a certain air of seriousness to her denunciation! Unfortunately, such seriousness does not seem to get through to those Americans who most need to hear and understand it.

Meanwhile Billy Graham declared that the war in Vietnam was a "spiritual war between good and evil." A plausible statement, certainly, but not in the way in which he meant it. At the same time a Saigon Catholic leader gave another view of the picture: "We are caught in struggle between two power blocs.... Many people told me you cannot trust Americans, but I never accepted it. Now I am beginning to believe it. You come to help my people, but they will hate you for it."

The tragic thing about Vietnam is that, after all, the "realism" of our program there is so unrealistic, so rooted in myth, so completely out of touch with the needs of the people whom we know only as statistics and to whom we never manage to listen, except where they fit in with our psychopathic delusions. Our external violence in Vietnam is rooted in an inner violence which simply ignores the human reality of those we claim to be helping. The result of this at home has been an ever-mounting desperation on the part of those who see the uselessness and inhumanity of the war, together with an increasing stubbornness and truculence on the part of those who insist they want to win, regardless of what victory may mean.

What will the situation be when this book appears in print? Will the 1968 presidential election force the issue one way or another? Will the candidates *have* to make sense out of this in spite of everything? We are getting to the point where American "victory" in Vietnam is becoming a word without any possible human meaning. What matters is the ability and willingness to arrive at some kind of workable solution that will save the identity of the nation that still wants to survive in spite of us, in spite of Communism, in spite of the international balance of power. This cannot be arrived at unless the United States is willing to deescalate, stop bombing the North, stop destroying crops, and recognize the NLF as among those with whom we have to deal if we want to make peace. Obviously a perfect solution is impossible but some solution can be realized and lives can be saved.

It is still possible to learn something from Vietnam: and above all we should recognize that the United States has received from no one the mission to police every country in the world or to decide for them how they are to live. No single nation has the right to try to run the world according to its own ideas. One thing is certain, the Vietnam war is a tragic error and, in the words of the resigned volunteers, "an overwhelming atrocity."

How do we explain such atrocities? Obviously, they are well-meant and the Americans who support the war are, for the most part, convinced that it is an inescapable moral necessity. Why? For one thing, as the more sophisticated reader is well aware, the picture of the war given by the mass media and the official version of what is happening are both extremely one-sided and oversimplified, to say the least. Some claim that the public has been deliberately misinformed. In any case, Americans do not seem to realize what effect the war is really having. The hatred of America which it is causing everywhere (analogous to the hatred of Russia after the violent suppression of the Hungarian revolt in 1956) is not just the result of Red propaganda. On the contrary, the Communists could never do such a fine job of blackening us as we are doing all by ourselves.

There is another, deeper source of delusion in the popular mythology of our time. One example of this popular mythology is examined in the first chapter of this section. It is the myth that all biological species in their struggle for survival must follow a law of aggression in which the stronger earns the right to exist by violently exterminating all his competitors. This pseudoscientific myth is simply another version of the cliché that "might makes right" and of course it was explicitly used and developed by the ideologists of Nazism. This canonization of violence by pseudoscience has come to be so much taken for granted, that when Konrad Lorenz in his carefully thought out study *On Aggression* sought to qualify it in very important ways, his book has simply been lumped with others, like Mr. Ardrey's, as one more rationalization of the aggression theory. Thus in the *New York Times Book Review* (Christmas issue, 67) the paperback edition of *On Aggression* is summarized with approval in this one line: "Like all other animals man is instinctively aggressive." True, of course, up to a point. But this contains the same implicit false conclusion ("therefore he *has* to beat up and destroy members of his own kind") and explicitly ignores the real point of Lorenz's book. The point is that man is the *only species,* besides the rat, who wantonly and cruelly turns on his own kind in *unprovoked* and murderous hostility. Man is the only one who deliberately seeks to *destroy* his own kind (as opposed to merely resisting encroachment).

To quote a prominent Dutch psychoanalyst who, among other things, has studied the mentality of Nazi war criminals:

> What we usually call hatred or hostility is different from normal self-assertive aggression. The former are hypercharged fantasy products, mixed with reactions to frustrations. They form an aura of intense anticipation of revenge and greater discharge in the future. . . . This finds its most paradoxical action in the hatred of those who want to break out into history. They destroy because they want to be remembered. NO OTHER ANIMAL AVAILS HIMSELF OF PLANS FOR MOBILIZATION AND FUTURE ATTACK. However, man gets caught in his own trap, and what he once dreamed up in a fatal hour takes possession of him so that he is finally compelled to act it out.

(I am grateful to my friend Dr. Joost A. M. Meerloo for permission to quote from his unpublished manuscript of the English version of *Homo Militans*.)

Now this develops the point made by Lorenz in *On Aggression*. Lorenz *distinguishes* the destructive hostility of men and of rats from the natural self-assertive aggression common to all species, and indicates that far from pointing to the "survival of the fittest" this drive toward intraspecific aggression may perhaps lead to the self-destruction of the human race. That is the thesis developed in detail by Dr. Meerloo. Mr. Ardrey's book, like so much other popular mythology on the subject, serves to contribute to those "hypercharged fantasies" by which modern man at once excuses and foments his inner hostilities until he is compelled to discharge them, as we are now doing, with immense cost for innocent and harmless people on the other side of the globe.

(I have examined elsewhere the psychological connection between the Indian wars of extermination in the last century, and the Vietnam war. See "Ishi: A Meditation," in the *Catholic Worker*, March 1967, and pages 113–125 in this volume.)

It is because of these obsessions and fantasies that we continue to draft our young men into the army when in fact a professional army of enlisted men would suffice, along with our fabulous nuclear arsenal, to meet any conceivable need for national defense. The Vietnam war has called the legality and justice of the draft law into question, and rightly. Our young men feel that they are simply being imposed upon and that their lives are being stupidly sacrificed, not to defend the country but to act out the manias of politicians and manufacturers who think they have a mission to police the world and run the affairs of smaller countries in the interests of American business. The draft law ought to be abolished. That would somewhat lessen the temptation to get involved in any more "overwhelming atrocities" like the one in Vietnam.

Eleven

Note for *Ave Maria*

This "Note," published in *Ave Maria* magazine in the issue of September 7, 1968, bore the original title: "Non-Violence Does Not…Cannot…Mean Passivity."

There seems to be a general impression that nonviolence in America has been tried and found wanting. The tragic death of Martin Luther King is supposed to have marked the end of an era in which nonviolence could have any possible significance, and the Poor People's March has been described as a sort of post mortem on nonviolence. From now on, we hear, it's violence only. Why? Because nonviolence not only does not get results, it is not even effective as communication.

I might as well say clearly that I do not believe this at all. And in spite of the fact that the Montgomery bus boycott, for instance, was a great example of the effective use of nonviolence both as tactic and as communication, in spite of the freedom rides, Birmingham, Selma, etc., I don't think America has yet begun to look at nonviolence or to really understand it. It is not my business to tell the SNCC people how to manage their political affairs. If they feel that they can no longer make good use of non-violence, let them look to it. There are certainly reasons for thinking that a seemingly passive resistance may not be what the Black people of America can profitably use. Nor do I think, incidentally, that "Black Power" means nothing but mindless and anarchic violence. It is more sophisticated than that.

But we are considering the Peace Movement.

The napalming of draft records by the Baltimore nine is a special and significant case because it seems to indicate a borderline situation: as if the Peace Movement too were standing at the very edge of violence. As if this were a sort of "last chance" at straight nonviolence and a first step toward violent resistance. Well, we live in a world of escalation in which no one seems to know how to deescalate, and it does pose a problem. The Peace Movement may be escalating beyond peaceful protest. In which case it may also be escalating into self-contradiction. But let me make it clear that I do not think the Baltimore nine have done this.

What were the Berrigans and the others trying to do?

It seems to me this was an attempt at prophetic non-violent provocation. It bordered on violence and was violent to the extent that it meant pushing some good ladies around and destroying some government property. The nine realized that this was a criminal act and knew that they could go to jail for it. They accepted this in the classic nonviolent fashion. The standard doctrine of nonviolence says that you can disobey a law you consider unjust but you have to accept the punishment. In this way you are distinguished from the mere revolutionary. You protest the purity of your witness. You undergo redemptive suffering for religious — or anyway ethical — motives. You are "doing penance" for the sin and injustice against which you have protested. And in the case of the Berrigans, I would say there is present a sort of "jail mystique," as a way of saying dumbly to the rest of the country that in our society nobody is really free anyway. That we are all prisoners of a machinery that takes us inevitably where we don't want to go. Presumably *everyone* in the country wants peace in one way or other. But most Americans have prior commitments — or attachments — to other things which make peace impossible. Most people would rather have war and profits than peace and problems. Or so it seems. In such a situation, we speak peace with our lips but the answer in the heart is war, and war only. And there is certain indecency involved when Christians, even prelates, canonize this unpleasant fact by saying that the war in Vietnam is an act of Christian love. Small wonder that certain more sensitive and more questioning people are driven to extremities.

The evident desperation of the Baltimore nine has, however, frightened more than it has edified. The country is in a very edgy psychological state. Americans feel terribly threatened, on grounds which are partly rational, partly irrational, but in any case very real. The rites of assassination recur at more and more frequent intervals, and there is less and less of a catharsis each time. The shocking thing about the murder of another Kennedy is that we seem to have such a terrible propensity to destroy the things and people we admire, the very ones we identify with. (I say, "we" insofar as we all have a real stake in the society which makes such things not only possible but easy.) There is, then, a real fear, a deep ambivalence, about our very existence and the order on which we think it depends. In such a case, the use of nonviolence has to be extremely careful and clear. People are not in a mood for clear thinking: their fears and premonitions have long ago run away with their minds before anyone can get to them with a cool nonviolent statement. And it has long ago become automatic to interpret nonviolence as violence merely because it is resistance.

The classic (Gandhian) doctrine of nonviolence, even in a much less tense and explosive situation, always emphasized respect for the just laws in order to highlight clearly and unambiguously the injustice of the unjust law. In this way, nonviolence did not pose a sort of free-floating psychological threat, but was clearly pinpointed, directed to what even the adversary had to admit was wrong. Ideally, that is what nonviolence is supposed to do. But if nonviolence merely says in a very loud voice *"I don't like this damn law,"* it does not do much to make the adversary admit that the law is wrong. On the contrary, what he sees is an apparently arbitrary attack on law and order, dictated by emotion or caprice — or fanaticism of some sort. His reply is obviously going to be: "Well, if you don't like law and order you can go to jail where you belong." And he will send you to jail with a firm and righteous conviction that the law is just. He will not even for a moment have occasion to question its justice. He will be too busy responding to what he feels to be aggressive and indignant in your near-violent protest.

It seems to me that the protest and resistance against the Selective Service Law is all oriented to the affirmation of the rightness, the determination, and the conviction of the protesters, and not to the injustice of the law itself. In other words, people who are protesting against the draft seem to be communicating, before everything else, their own intense conviction that the law is wrong, rather than pointing out where and how the law is wrong. It boils down to saying, "We don't like this law and feel strongly that it is bad." To which the opposition is content to reply: "The real reason why you don't like the draft is that you are a coward."

What is to be done? First, on a short-term and emergency basis, the whole Vietnam problem has to be solved even if it demands a certain political compromise. It is idiotic to hold out for negotiations in which the position of the other side is completely ignored. Senator McCarthy seems to me to be the only presidential candidate who has the remotest idea of how to end the war, and he is the only one for whom I personally, in conscience, can vote. The war being ended, I think it is necessary that we realize the draft law is unjust, useless, and an occasion of further interference in the affairs of small countries we cannot understand. It should be abolished. It has no relation to the real defense needs of the country. On a long-term basis, I think the Peace Movement needs to really study, practice, and use nonviolence in its classic form, with all that this implies of religious and ethical grounds. The current facile rejection of nonviolence is too pragmatic. You point to one or two cases where it does not seem to have got results and you say it has completely failed.

But nonviolence is useless if it is merely pragmatic. The whole point of nonviolence is that it rises above pragmatism and does not consider whether or not it pays off officially. *Ahimsa* is defense of and witness to *truth*, not efficacy. I admit that may sound odd. Someone once said, did he not, "What is truth?" And the One to whom he said it also mentioned, somewhere: "The truth shall make you free." It seems to me that this is what really matters.

– Appendix –

Merton's Prayer for Peace

This prayer, written by Thomas Merton, was read in the House of Representatives by Congressman Frank Kowalski (D-Conn.) on April 12, 1962, the Wednesday in Holy Week.

Almighty and merciful God, Father of all men, Creator and Ruler of the Universe, Lord of History, whose designs are inscrutable, whose glory is without blemish, whose compassion for the errors of men is inexhaustible, in your will is our peace.

Mercifully hear this prayer which rises to you from the tumult and desperation of a world in which you are forgotten, in which your name is not invoked, your laws are derided and your presence is ignored. Because we do not know you, we have no peace.

From the heart of an eternal silence, you have watched the rise of empires, and seen the smoke of their downfall.

You have seen Egypt, Assyria, Babylon, Greece and Rome, once powerful, carried away like sand in the wind.

166

You have witnessed the impious fury of ten thousand
fratricidal wars, in which great powers have torn
whole continents to shreds in the name of peace and
justice.

And now our nation itself stands in imminent danger of
a war the like of which has never been seen!

This nation dedicated to freedom, not to power,

Has obtained, through freedom, a power it did not desire.

And seeking by that power to defend its freedom, it is
enslaved by the processes and policies of power.

Must we wage a war we do not desire, a war that can do
us no good,

And which our very hatred of war forces us to prepare?

A day of ominous decision has now dawned on this free
nation.

Armed with a titanic weapon, and convinced of our own
right,

We face a powerful adversary, armed with the same
weapon, equally convinced that he is right.

In this moment of destiny, this moment we never foresaw,
we cannot afford to fail.

Our choice of peace or war may decide our judgment
and publish it in an eternal record.

In this fatal moment of choice in which we might begin
the patient architecture of peace.

We may also take the last step across the rim of chaos.

Save us then from our obsessions! Open our eyes,
dissipate confusions, teach us to understand ourselves
and our adversary!

Let us never forget that sins against the law of love are
punished by loss of faith,

And those without faith stop at no crime to achieve their
ends!

Help us to be masters of the weapons that threaten to
master us.

Help us to use our science for peace and plenty, not for
war and destruction.

Show us how to use atomic power to bless our children's
children, not to blight them.

Save us from the compulsion to follow our adversaries in
all that we most hate, confirming them in their hatred
and suspicion of us.

Resolve our inner contradictions, which now grow
beyond belief and beyond bearing.

They are at once a torment and a blessing: for if you had
not left us the light of conscience, we would not have
to endure them.

Teach us to be long-suffering in anguish and insecurity.

Teach us to wait and trust.

Grant light, grant strength and patience to all who work
for peace,

To this Congress, our President, our military forces, and our adversaries.
Grant us prudence in proportion to our power,
Wisdom in proportion to our science,
Humaneness in proportion to our wealth and might.
And bless our earnest will to help all races and peoples to travel, in friendship with us,
Along the road to justice, liberty and lasting peace:
But grant us above all to see that our ways are not necessarily your ways,
That we cannot fully penetrate the mystery of your designs
And that the very storm of power now raging on this earth
Reveals your hidden will and your inscrutable decision.
Grant us to see your face in the lightning of this cosmic storm,
O God of holiness, merciful to men:
Grant us to seek peace where it is truly found!

> *In your will, O God, is our peace!*
> *Amen*

Index

Index

171

Index

Of Related Interest

Gil Bailie
VIOLENCE UNVEILED
Humanity at the Crossroads

Introduction by René Girard

Winner of the Pax Christi–USA Book Award

This invaluable book provides a practical roadmap for the journey of forgiveness — a step-by-step process for healing, for freedom, for peace. Bailie's work is a must-read for those who wish to understand the nature of violence, as well as conceptualize a proactive Christian response.

"Anyone concerned about the rise of violence and social disintegration in our culture, and who wants to understand what is really happening, must read this book. It's that important."   — *Sojourners*

"The single most important book of social analysis and prophetic theology to appear in our generation."
— Sam Keen

0-8245-1645-1, $24.95, paperback

crossroad

Of Related Interest

Henri Nouwen
FINDING MY WAY HOME
Pathways to Life and the Spirit

A collection of four essays, three previously published by Crossroad and here revised, that examines four different aspects of our spiritual life: the Path of Waiting, the Path of Power, the Path of Peace, and the Path of Living and Dying (never before published in book form).

0-8245-1888-8, $18.95, hardcover

Check your local bookstore for availability.
To order directly from the publisher,
please call 1-800-707-0670 for Customer Service
or visit our Web site at *www.cpcbooks.com.*
For catalog orders, please send your request
to the address below.

THE CROSSROAD PUBLISHING COMPANY
16 Penn Plaza, Suite 1550
New York, NY 10001

All prices subject to change.

crossroad